Fast Class

The skills-based FCE/B2 course for exam success

STUDENT'S BOOK

Kathy Gude

OXFORD

UNIVERSITY PRESS

Contents

Use of English skills	Listening skills	Speaking skills	Revise and extend
Sports **Part 1** Multiple-choice cloze Modals	**A variety of topics** **Part 1** Multiple choice Words with different meanings	**Talking about yourself** **Part 1** Personal information Giving suitable answers	**page 12**
Birds and the environment **Part 1** Multiple-choice cloze The future	**A variety of topics** **Part 1** Multiple choice Words which sound the same	**Expressing likes and dislikes** **Part 1** Personal information Talking about likes dislikes and preferences	**page 22**
Language Present tenses Using adverbs **Part 2** Open cloze	Marine life **Part 2** Sentence completion Improving your spelling	Relationships **Part 2** The long turn Explaining what you mean	**page 32**
Personal experiences Past tenses Active and passive forms **Part 2** Open cloze	People and sport **Part 2** Sentence completion Words in context	Health and exercise **Part 2** The long turn Using comparatives and superlatives	**page 42**
The music industry The present perfect **Part 3** Key word transformations	**The arts** **Part 2** Note-taking Spelling: the *schwa* sound	**The media** **Part 2** The long turn Comparing photographs	**page 52**
History Relative clauses and pronouns **Part 3** Key word transformations	**A personal journey** **Part 2** Note-taking Predicting what you will hear	**Freetime activities** **Part 2** The long turn (a group of three) Words with similar meanings	**page 62**
Emergency services **Part 4** Error correction The past perfect Past perfect simple or continuous? Find the extra word	Transport and the environment **Part 3** Multiple matching Focusing on key words	Happiness **Parts 3 and 4** The collaborative task and discussion Starting a conversation Inviting your partner to speak	**page 72**
The weather **Part 4** Error correction Conditionals: zero, first, second and third	Friends and family **Part 3** Multiple matching Different words, the same meaning	The world in danger **Parts 3 and 4** The collaborative task and discussion Expressing your own opinion Making a suggestion	**page 82**
Holidays **Part 5** Word formation Wishes and regrets	Places to shop **Part 4** Three possible answers Listening for ideas expressed in different ways	Jobs and skills **Parts 3 and 4** The collaborative task and discussion Reaching a decision Agreeing to disagree	**page 92**
Fashion **Part 5** Word formation Reported speech	Entertainment **Part 4** A choice of two options Different spellings, similar sounds	Places to live **Parts 3 and 4** The collaborative task and discussion (a group of three) Inviting both partners to speak Interrupting politely	**page 102**

Reading skills

PART 1 MATCHING HEADINGS

1 Describe the differences between the picnics in the pictures. Have you ever been on picnics like these?

2 Read the article quickly, ignoring the missing headings. Find six things that might spoil a picnic.

3 Choose the most suitable heading from the list A–I for each part (1–7) of the article. There is one extra heading which you do not need to use.

A Sad but unfortunately true
B Willing to accept that anywhere will do
C Bigger is definitely better
D Unplanned but more likely to succeed
E Unreal but unforgettable
F Luxurious and worth the effort
G Soaked but happy with the simple life
H Disappointed but cheered up by the meal
I Determined in spite of the problems

Negative prefixes

4 The writer uses the word *unplanned* in heading D. Write words which mean the opposite of those in a–j using the prefixes *un*, *im*, *in* or *dis*, and use five of them in sentences of your own.

a perfect   f like (adjective)
b appear   g correct (adjective)
c fasten   h necessary
d ripe   i expensive
e like (verb)   j real

Noun endings

5 Find three nouns in the article that end with *-ion*. Then use one of the endings below to make the noun forms of adjectives a–h. You may need to change other letters in the words.

-ion	-ity	-ment	-ness
-y	-ation	-action	

a real   e unwilling
b perfect   f generous
c disappointed   g satisfying
d determined   h luxurious

---

0 | *I* |

In some countries picnics are a way of life. We British were never meant to picnic but we battle on, regardless of the wind, rain and thick cloud that appears quicker than you c[a] unfasten the leather straps on a picnic basket. Regardless o[f]
5 nettles and wasps' nests, and of barbed wire. We know that fresh air sharpens the appetite and lifts the spirits. Sunshin[e] and a light breeze can make even a sandwich twice the me[a] it is indoors. In short, food tastes better outdoors. But there is more to it than that. The need to picnic is part of our
10 culture and nothing is going to stop us.

The perfect picni[c]

1 | |

The perfect picnic exists only in a far off corner of our min[d] an escape, a place to go and daydream. We never have, and almost certainly never will have, that idyllic outdoor meal on a tartan rug by a babbling stream, because as they say, it[']
15 all in the mind. What is so mystifying is the similarity between everyone's memories of the perfect picnic. So just when did we experience that magical meal in a buttercup-strewn meadow? And how come we can remember every la[st] detail of it when we know very well that it never actually
20 happened?

2 | |

The reasons not to picnic are outnumbered only by the several good reasons why we should. For every hornets' nes[t] and forgotten corkscrew there are twice as many melting cheeses and sweet, ripe tomatoes for us to put in our basket[.]
25 Each beauty spot littered with abandoned fridges is easily outnumbered by the thought of loaves of crusty bread and slices of cool melon. In other words, it is the food that save[s] the day. Get that right, and nothing short of a tidal wave c[an] dampen our enthusiasm.

3

30 If it is to have a hope of turning out right, however, a picnic must be a snap decision. So, rule number one is never set a date weeks in advance. Picnics are part
35 of life in countries with a steady climate. In Britain, they tend to depend totally on what the sky is doing on the day. Which means doing nothing until the last
40 minute, like it or not.

4

Then we must find that secret spot. The correct location isn't everything. We can spread out our cloth in a lay-by if we must. We have been led to believe that it is necessary to picnic in an English meadow. But with one half of the
45 countryside under a blanket of yellow rape-seed fields, and the other half turned into golf courses, we can no longer be so fussy. Hardened picnickers know that every place big enough to unpack a basket is fair game.

5

50 I have to admit that I have a soft spot for rained-out picnics. Not out of a sense of spite, but because I like the smell of sandwiches, drenched dogs and flasks of coffee in a damp car. Nostalgia no doubt, but it is as fine a seasoning for a meal as salt and pepper. As far as I am concerned, five
55 people in a car passing around packets of cheese and onion crisps and chunks of meat pie is far more fun than pushing a china plate of expensive food around a white linen picnic cloth.

6

But you must be generous. No one will thank you for that miserable tub of dip and packet of pitta bread you
60 picked up at the corner shop. There must be plenty to eat. A whole cheese costs less than lots of small bits and looks vastly more interesting. A huge bowl of cherries will make ten times the impression of a chopped up fruit salad. Think on a large scale, but think simple.

7

65 If all this sounds a bit like battle plans, then it is only because that's what we will need. We can organise the food, the location and the friends. We can pack our picnic
70 with care and even remember the mustard, but we need to remember also that we are dealing with something bigger than us all: the simple fact that the British were never born to eat outdoors.

Text talk...

◆ What overall point is the writer making about picnics?

◆ What do you think you need to make a picnic perfect?

Exam know-how

Paper 1 Part 1

● Read all the paragraphs quickly for gist.
● Don't worry about the meanings of individual words in the paragraphs as you may not need to understand them to do the task.
● Read the headings carefully and think about their possible meanings.
● Read the paragraphs again carefully to identify what each paragraph is about.
● Try every heading in each gap. Remember the heading will not repeat exactly what is in the text.
● Try the unused heading in each gap once more.

HELP

The phrasal verb *pick up*

6 What does *picked up* in line 60 mean? Match the other uses of *pick up* in 1–4 with explanations a–d.

a learn
b improve
c come/go and fetch
d take hold of and lift

1 Could you pick up that box and carry it to the car, please?
2 David has picked up French really quickly.
3 Business always picks up when the tourists start to arrive.
4 Could you pick me up from the tube station this evening?

7 Complete these sentences using the phrasal verb *pick up* in the correct form, and your own words.

a Would you mind .... me .... from .... ?
b Whatever you do, don't try to .... It's far too heavy for you.
c We're hoping that trade .... when .... in the summer.
d When I lived in Spain, I .... the language quickly because ....

Writing skills

PART 1 INFORMAL TRANSACTIONAL LETTER

1 Read the question and the postcard opposite, ignoring the notes Carla has made, and find out
   a why David has sent the postcard.
   b what he would like Carla to do.
   c what he is looking forward to.
   d what he wants to know.

2 Which of the following is David doing in the postcard? What words and expressions does he use to do these things?
   a giving information
   b requesting information
   c making a complaint
   d asking for advice
   e making a suggestion
   f making a request

3 Find informal words or expressions David uses which mean the same as these more formal ones.
   a telephone you
   b waste time waiting for
   c very excited at the thought of
   d similar kinds of things
   e Can you give me any information about

4 Look at the notes Carla has made on David's postcard. What do you think she is going to say in her letter in reply? Write one sentence for each of her notes.

5 Read Carla's letter on the opposite page. Is it different from what you expected? Use the Writing checklist to help you.

Your cousin is coming to stay with you for a week. Read his postcard, on which you have made some notes. Using all the information in your notes, write a suitable reply of between 120 and 180 words in an appropriate style. Do not write any addresses.

Hi, Carla! Just a postcard to say I'll be arriving at the end of next month. Could you meet me? Perhaps I can give you a ring about half an hour before I get there so you won't have to hang around for me. Can't wait to see the sights and have a few nights out together. By the way, what sort of clothes should I bring? Will we need swimming things or anything like that? Let me know. What about money? Is everything very expensive or can I get by without breaking the bank?
See you soon,
         David

What day? (have classes on weekdays)

take taxi?/ mention cost

summer/July usually warm

Which sights/ what to do?

need lots!

not interested in sport!

Writing checklist

All points covered/reader fully informed ☐
Well-organised layout ☐
Ideas linked clearly ☐
Appropriate style ☐
Suitable opening and closing ☐
Grammar and spelling correct ☐
The right vocabulary for the task ☐
The right length ☐
Legible handwriting ☐

LONDON

Dear my cousin,

I need to know if you are coming by bus or train and when you arriving. It is difficult to meet you because I have class until 6.30. You will have to take a taxi to my house. You mention to see the sights but not which sights. I don't like to staying out too late at night so we have to think of something for earlier in the evening. Clothes are not a problem. You can wear what you like. I don't like swiming so we won't go swiming. I am exciting that you are coming because we have not see each other since a long time.
Yours sincerely,

carla

HELP

Paper 2 Part 1
- You must answer the Part 1 question. It has equal marks with Part 2 so allow enough time for both.
- Read the input material carefully so that you include everything in the question.
- Use the right tone for the person reading your letter.
- Use a different paragraph for each new idea.
- Check your finished letter for sense and errors.
- Don't waste time counting every word. Estimate the number of words to a line and count the number of lines.

Can you tell me ... ?

6   What changes do you need to make to the question *Are you coming by train?* to begin *Can you tell me .... ?* Rewrite a–h in the same way. You may need to make other changes to the sentences.

a What time does your train arrive?
b Which hotel are you staying at?
c Where should I meet you?
d Do you need somewhere to stay?
e What would you like to do?
f Are you interested in opera?
g Would you like to go on a river trip?
h When are you thinking of going home?

Expressions with *way*

7   Find an expression with *way* in David's postcard. What does it mean? Complete sentences a–f using *way* and the words below.

| in my   a long   get her own |
| out of their   find your   on our |

a I hope you can .... to my house.
b I live .... from the airport.
c .... home, we can do some sight-seeing.
d My host family went .... to make me feel at home.
e I'm sorry but your suitcases are ....
f My sister always likes to ....

Writing a reply

8   Read the question in 1 and the notes on the postcard
HELP   again, then write your own reply to David. Think about what was wrong with Carla's letter, and try to use some of the structures and expressions in 6 and 7. The Writing checklist on page 6 will help you.

Use of English skills

PART 1 MULTIPLE-CHOICE CLOZE

1 Read the text quickly ignoring the spaces, and
find out what the X-Games are.

Is this really sport?

What, in your 0 .... , might 'alternative sports with
attitude' be? Judging by yesterday afternoon's TV coverage of the
X-Games, they 1 .... be what we traditionally term sport because
they 2 .... young people in baggy shorts going at very high
3 .... down ramps and doing fancy turnovers. They do this on
skateboards, BMX bikes or roller skates, which are now called in-line skates to
4 .... them sound more sporty. I accept the fact that sports 5 ....
these are very popular with young people – so 6 .... so that many
youngsters think of them more as 7 .... with birthday presents than as
actual sport. But surely those youngsters, on a warm and sunny Saturday
afternoon, would have been better off if they had 8 .... part in proper
sports of their own? What the programme 9 .... to have given viewers
was more clarification of the criteria by which these show-off competitors
were being judged. I did not 10 .... , for example, how they could
11 .... on their bikes and skates and still 12 .... the gold medal.
Were they perhaps being given extra points for the number of unnecessary
pockets on their shorts? The presenter of the X-Games 13 .... us that in-
line skating was 'all about free expression'. The inconvenient thing about sport,
14 .... , is that it tends to be about discipline, about excellence within
clearly set guidelines, not about 'free expression'. What she was 15 ....
is more like ballet dancing or modern jazz!

FOCUS ON MODALS

Test your knowledge

Which of these statements about
modals are true?

a They have no continuous forms.
b They have past forms.
c They are never followed by *to*.
d They are always used with
   another verb.
e They are used to express feelings
   or attitudes.
f They have -s in the third person
   singular.
g They can be used in question tags.
h They always form their negative
   by adding *not*.

can, could, be able to

3 In which of a–j do the modals
indicate: possibility, ability, a polite
request, a suggestion, permission?

a Could you speak English when
   you were five years old?
b Can you come swimming?
c Could you tell me the time?
d We could go to the cinema.
e I could feel the warm wind.
f You can leave work early today
   as there's very little to do.
g That could be true.
h I suppose Greg could have
   forgotten our telephone
   number.
i Were you able to ride a bike
   when you were a child?
j I could meet you for lunch.

2 For questions 1–15, read the text again and decide which answer (A, B, C
or D) best fits each space.

0 A idea	B belief	C mind	(D) opinion
1 A must	B would	C mightn't	D can't
2 A contained	B included	C enclosed	D concerned
3 A rush	B hurry	C speed	D haste
4 A do	B make	C cause	D result
5 A like	B as	C such	D so
6 A many	B much	C far	D largely
7 A acting	B amusing	C playing	D enjoying
8 A taken	B had	C been	D performed
9 A might	B should	C ought	D could
10 A understand	B guess	C imagine	D realise
11 A fall off	B fall through	C fall over	D fall out
12 A beat	B win	C succeed	D catch
13 A explained	B mentioned	C said	D told
14 A even	B however	C although	D yet
15 A describing	B talking	C meaning	D commenting

must be/have been, can't be/have been

4 Complete a–e using one of the forms.

  a You .... feeling well. You haven't eaten your dinner.

  b Phil .... exhausted yesterday. He ran in the marathon.

  c You .... Brian's new flatmate. He told me you'd moved in last week.

  d It .... possibly .... six o'clock already. Where has the day gone?

  e Who broke this window? It .... the children because they've gone to school.

must/mustn't, have/had to

5 Use one of the forms to complete a–e. More than one answer may be possible. How would you put the first sentence into the past? (Be careful as you need to use another verb!)

  a Students .... smoke in the library. It's forbidden.

  b I .... send my grandmother a card. She'll be really upset if I forget her birthday.

  c When we arrived at the airport we .... hire a car because there was no one there to meet us.

  d .... we .... hand in this homework tomorrow, or can we have more time?

  e I .... get up early this morning to catch the train. I had an important meeting.

may/might (not), can/could (not)

6 Which of the modals could you use to complete a–e? How would the meaning change depending on the modals you used?

  a It .... rain this afternoon. There are some dark clouds over there.

  b .... I use your phone?

  c Paul .... not have received my call.

  d We .... be able to come to your party.

  e You .... leave your luggage at the reception desk for as long as you like.

mustn't, needn't, (not) have to

7 Which of the modals can have the same meaning? Complete a–c using them in the correct form.

  a You .... do the homework tonight. You can hand it in on Friday.

  b You .... be late for work on your first day. It creates a very bad impression.

  c We .... buy train tickets at the station tomorrow because they sell them on board.

Exam know-how

Paper 3 Part 1

- Look carefully at the title for an idea of what the text is about.
- Read the text quickly for gist.
- When you have chosen your answer, try all the other options to make sure they don't fit.
- Read each completed sentence in your head to check meaning and grammar.

should/ought to (do/have done)

8 Use one of these verbs and the words in brackets in the correct form to complete a–f.

> spend   go   remember
> be   begin   leave

  a We .... (should) to look for a hotel much earlier. We'll never find one now!

  b The plane .... (ought) by now. It was due to leave ten minutes ago.

  c We .... (ought) somewhere different for our holidays. We were bored doing the same things.

  d The children .... (should) in bed now. It's nearly nine o'clock.

  e You .... (should) to phone your parents last night. They'll be worried.

  f Sam .... (ought) more time doing his homework if he wants to pass the exam.

didn't need to, didn't have to, needn't have

9 Decide which of the phrases in italics below means *We did this although it wasn't necessary*, then complete sentences a–d using one of the phrases and the verb in brackets.

- We *needn't have rushed* to catch the train because it was cancelled.
- We *didn't need to pay* to get into the exhibition because it was free.
- We *didn't have to do* any homework last night because the teacher didn't set any.

  a My brother .... (take) a taxi after the party because someone gave him a lift home.

  b It was kind of you to telephone but you .... (go) to all that trouble.

  c I .... (be) at school until 10.30 yesterday morning so I had a lie-in.

  d We .... (worry) about being late because when we got there no other guests had arrived.

Listening skills

PART 1   MULTIPLE CHOICE
Words with different meanings

1 Read the questions and options in 2 below. Decide which meaning, a or b, is most likely for these words from each extract.

1 past
   a long ago
   b after

2 flight
   a a series of steps
   b journey by plane

3 in the way of
   a be an obstacle
   b regarding

4 order
   a request
   b command

5 the nerve
   a a part of the body
   b the courage

6 unwind
   a undo
   b take it easy

7 customs
   a ways of behaving
   b officials at borders

8 company
   a business or firm
   b being with a person

2 🎧 You will hear people talking in eight different situations.

HELP For questions 1–8, choose the best answer, A, B or C.

1 A couple who have just moved house are talking to each other. What is the man complaining about?
   A moving the furniture
   B having to unpack
   C missing lunch

2 You hear a tourist guide talking about some old town houses. Who were they built for?

   A the general public
   B company employees
   C people without servants

3 A woman approaches you outside a railway station. What does she want you to do now?

   A give her some personal details
   B fill in a questionnaire
   C take part in a survey

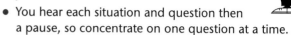
4 You hear the recorded message of a holiday company. What can you do if you press 'two'?

   A ask for a brochure
   B speak to an operator
   C enquire about a previous booking

5 You hear part of a radio interview with an author. How does the author feel?

   A bitter
   B misunderstood
   C nervous

6 A doctor is talking about long-distance flying. What does she say passengers should do?

   A keep to their normal routine
   B eat little when on board
   C relax after landing

7 While at the post office, you hear a man talking. What is he worried about?

   A the cost of posting his parcel
   B how to send his parcel
   C losing his parcel

8 You hear an advertisement on the radio. What is special about the products on offer?

   A They are good value.
   B They are easy to handle.
   C They are elegant.

3 🎧 Which meaning did the words in 1 have?

What about you?

4 Answer these questions.

   a Have you ever moved house? What problems did you have?
   b Would you like to do a lot of long-distance flying? Why/Why not?
   c Have you ever bought something advertised on the radio or TV? What?

Speaking skills

PART 1 PERSONAL INFORMATION

1 Tick the subjects you think the examiner might ask you about in this first part of the speaking test.

a home ☐

b neighbourhood ☐

c family ☐

d environmental problems ☐

e future plans ☐

f making decisions ☐

g plans for the weekend ☐

h hobbies and interests ☐

i comparing photos ☐

j jobs ☐

k studying English ☐

l your partner's photographs ☐

m past experiences ☐

n feelings ☐

Giving suitable answers

2 These sentences all contain at least one mistake. Say them correctly.

a I am coming from the Spain.

b I was grown up in city.

c I live at the very large flat.

d I'm student of the history at the university.

e My family is quite as small – just my mother and father, and by myself, of course.

f I am enjoying to live in my neighbourhood.

g If I would, I could live close at the seaside.

h I've been study English since six years.

i My brother speak Spanish fluent.

j I like very much the sports, on particular, tennis.

3 Look again at the sentences you corrected in 2. What questions would you ask to find out this information?

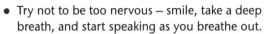

Exam know-how

Paper 5 Part 1

- Try not to be too nervous – smile, take a deep breath, and start speaking as you breathe out.
- Don't take too long before answering.
- Speak loudly and clearly enough for both examiners to hear you.
- If you don't understand the question, ask the examiner to repeat it.
- If you have no plans, interest or hobbies, etc., explain why, e.g. 'because I have no time'.
- Don't use the same words repeatedly.

4 Read this conversation between a candidate and an examiner. Why are Pierre's answers unsuitable? How could they be improved?

A *Pierre, do you live in town?*

B *No.*

A *Where are you from?*

B *A village.*

A *What do you like about living there?*

B *I like it.*

5 With a partner, use the subjects you ticked in 1 to ask and answer questions about yourselves. Expand on your answers with an extra piece of information.

HELP

Example: *I live in a flat. It's a big flat on the second floor and it has a lovely balcony where we all sit in summer.*

Revise and extend

Negative prefixes

▶ Revision p4 Ex4

1 Match the negative prefixes with a–h, then use the words in the correct form to complete 1–8.

> un-   im-   in-   dis-

a patient   d polite   g comfortable
b necessary   e advantage   h correct
c appear   f convenient

1 22 + 22 = 45 is a(n) .... answer.
2 This new sofa is extremely .... to sit on. It isn't big enough.
3 Pete is a very .... driver. He's always losing his temper.
4 My new pen has .... Have you seen it by any chance?
5 Being too rich can be a(n) .... Some people only like you for your money!
6 Is it considered .... in your country to use the first name of people you've just met?
7 We could have a meeting on Saturday if that isn't too .... for you.
8 Do we need to do any more revision on this topic? It seems a bit .... to me!

Expressions with *pick*

▶ Extension p5 Ex6

2 Match meanings a–e with the verbs in 1–5.

a pick on someone
b pick someone's pocket
c pick a fight or quarrel
d pick up speed
e pick your way

1 cause an argument with someone deliberately
2 move slowly or carefully avoiding obstacles
3 criticise someone unfairly
4 steal money from someone's clothing
5 go faster

3 Use one of the verbs from 2 in its correct form to complete sentences a–e.

a I don't like Brian. He's always trying to .... with the other boys in the class.
b The car .... as it travelled down the hill.
c You shouldn't .... people who are weaker than you are.
d Someone .... on the train yesterday and stole all my money.
e The children .... across the beach, which was covered in pebbles.

Words and meanings

▶ Revision p4/5 Text

4 Match phrases a–e with the meanings in the box, then use a–e to complete sentences 1–5. More than one answer may be possible

> in my opinion   I'm certain   to summarise
> I have to confess   to put it another way

a in short
b in other words
c no doubt
d I have to admit
e as far as I'm concerned

1 .... it will be raining tomorrow. It always does when we go for a picnic!
2 .... , I'm terrified of spiders!
3 The journey was long, tiring and uncomfortable; .... , it was dreadful.
4 .... that I don't really like Jim. He never listens to a word anybody says.
5 .... , watching a performance of a play in the rain is madness!

5 Make nouns a–f into adjectives and use them to complete sentences 1–6.

a similarity
b success
c necessity
d fuss
e nostalgia
f misery

1 I felt really .... yesterday. I think it was because of the terrible weather.
2 Just eat what's on your plate. You shouldn't be so .... about food.
3 I don't think that homework was really .... because I already knew those words.
4 Is the climate in your country .... to the weather here?
5 I often feel .... when I look back on my childhood.
6 Jane became a very .... computer engineer. She earned a lot of money.

Writing

▶ Extension p4/5

6 Your class have decided to hold an end-of-term picnic 'with a difference'. Write an invitation to be sent to friends, family and teachers. Include: place, date, time, what to bring, who to reply to. Remember to say why your picnic is going to be different, and include an alternative plan for what to do if the weather is bad.

Can you tell me ... ?

▶ Revision p7 Ex6

7 Rewrite a–f beginning *Can you tell me ... ?*

a Where's the railway station?

b What are you going to study at university?

c Who are you writing to?

d Are you going to the seminar on Saturday?

e Would you like to study another language?

f Do you like opera?

Modal verbs

▶ Revision p8/9

8 Use the verb in brackets and a suitable modal to complete these sentences.

a Unfortunately my boyfriend (go) on holiday with us next year.

b We (revise) for our exams instead of watching TV.

c What (do) about the rise in the number of crimes?

d This food in the fridge (eat) yesterday. It's past its sell-by date!

e You (listen) when I explained what to do because you have done something completely different.

f This picture (paint) by Picasso. I'm sure of it.

g You really (buy) me a present but it was kind of you.

h Everyone (try) to concentrate more in class.

9 Correct the mistakes in these sentences.

a Students might on no account be late for lessons.

b Ted might have get held up in the traffic. He's never usually late.

c We couldn't be able to go to the cinema tomorrow.

d Luggage must not to be left unattended.

e We could have gone out for a pizza if you'd like to.

f Do we must finish this homework by tomorrow?

g We didn't need to be nervous. The exam was easy.

h When I woke up, I can hear the birds singing.

i I didn't had to wait long for a train last night.

j I don't know where Rob is. I suppose he should have taken his dog for a walk.

10 Put a line through the modals which cannot be used in these sentences.

a You *must/ought/can't* be tired!

b It *can/might/may* snow tomorrow.

c We *have to/need/must* get up early tomorrow.

d My aunt *should/must/had to* have had her operation by now.

e You *should/could/can* have come to stay with us last weekend when you were in town.

f The students *didn't need to/didn't have to/needn't have* worried about their end-of-term test. They all got high marks.

▶ Extension p8/9

11 Use appropriate question tags to complete these sentences.

a Sky diving can be dangerous, ... ?

b You will come skiing with me, ... ?

c Ted could have phoned, ... ?

d Mary shouldn't have said that, ... ?

e Richard had to leave the party early, ... ?

f We didn't need to write two compositions, ... ?

g We must have missed the bus, ... ?

h Your parents might have phoned while we were out, ... ?

i Paul can't be serious about going to live in Australia for good, ... ?

Personal information

▶ Revision p11

12 Write questions to find out this information from someone you have just met.

a where/come from?

b where/grow up?

c where/live now?

d how long/live there?

e how long/study English?

f brothers or sisters?

g favourite sports?

h have interests/hobbies?

Reading skills

PART 1 MATCHING SUMMARY SENTENCES

1 In some countries, students do a few weeks' work experience while still at school. Decide how useful you think this is and what you could learn from it.

2 Read the article quickly, ignoring the missing summary sentences, and find five things the writer learned from his work experience in France.

3 Choose from the list A–I the sentence which best summarises each part (1–7) of the article. There is one extra sentence which you do not need to use.

CHECK

A Henry begins to be absorbed into French culture.
B Henry feels that he has survived an extremely worthwhile experience.
C Henry wonders if he is learning the right things.
D Henry finds he can cope in unexpected surroundings.
E Henry admits to being somewhat disappointed after realising his ambition.
F Henry discovers that life in France has its good points.
G Henry learns of a change of plan.
H Henry is not missing his family and friends.
I Henry realises he has underestimated the task ahead.

Phrasal verbs with *take*

4 What does *take up* (line 37) mean? The wrong phrasal verbs with *take* have been used in sentences a–f. Correct them, then match them with meanings 1–6.

a The teacher spoke so quickly that I couldn't take after what he was saying.
b This homework is taking in too much of my weekend.
c Don't you think Lisa takes away her mother?
d What do you get if you take seven back from ten?
e I think I will take these shoes off to the shop. They don't fit properly.
f I hear that an American company is taking to the organisation.

1 occupy (space or time)
2 subtract
3 follow or understand
4 get control of
5 resemble
6 return

Hold the front hoof!

How 17-year-old Henry Bainton's work experience at a French local newspaper turned into a crash course in farming.

0 | **I**

As Portsmouth drifted into the horizon, it seemed as if almost every useful word of French I had ever learned was left behind. What little that remained was shrinking as fast as the docks were fading into
5 obscurity. It dawned on me that this was really the point of no return. The very next day I would be working in France, writing in French on a local newspaper and living with a family that was not my own.

1

10 I was well prepared for my stay – my suit was pressed, my shoes polished, and my white shirts meticulously ironed. A hint of suspicion crept in though, when having arrived in the picturesque town of Flers where we were based, my teacher tactfully informed
15 me that there was a minor hitch. There had been a slight problem with the computers at the newspaper. 'Never mind,' I thought. 'I've already had some experience of a newsroom in England and I'm sure a French newsroom can't be that different so I won't be
20 missing too much.' 'You have brought your wellies though, haven't you?' asked the teacher.

2

I had little more with me than a suit carrier and a toothbrush. And so it was to my surprise that early the next day I found myself sheepishly standing in a
25 farmyard in hastily borrowed clothes and boots two sizes too big. This was the replacement placement – a farm. I felt like the new boy in the class all over again – a multitude of unfamiliar faces passively staring at me with an air of superiority. I had never been in
30 such close proximity to a cow before but I conceded in the

end that they were far less bothered by me than I was by them, and realised that a peaceful co-existence would probably be possible.

3 [ ]

35 It was arranged that work would start at a reasonable hour of the day. In rural France, there is no tea break at eleven, the lunch hour takes up twice as long – and starts an hour earlier. Nor was lunch just a sandwich at the canteen – only the farm's own roast meat,
40 home-made patisserie and home-brewed cider would suffice after a morning in the fields.

4 [ ]

Having aspired from the age of three to drive a tractor, I finally made it aboard the farm's latest purchase, a £300,000 Lamborghini. But I discovered
45 that it is really not all it is cracked up to be, and no more exciting than driving a car. My mind boggled at the complexity and cost of the gleaming new machine whose engine roared with so much as a tap on the gas pedal.

5 [ ]

50 French customs felt progressively less alien as the week went on. The whole ordeal of either kissing or shaking hands with everybody but the dog became routine. And I even found myself developing an interest in French sporting successes and fashions.

6 [ ]

55 Spending all that time with French teenagers, immersed in the language, meant taking in all those words that would shock my bilingual teacher. I am sure that come my oral exam in the summer, they will be the only words I can recall. By the end of the week,
60 I was dreaming in French.

7 [ ]

So it was a sigh of both relief and pathos that I breathed when we last steamed away from Caen. I had made it through a week that had started in the worst possible way and seemed destined to get even
65 worse. And above all, I learned a great deal – not only the hundred or so different expressions to shout at a misbehaving dog, but I also gained a genuine impression
70 of how the French live.

Text talk . . .

- How would you feel if you were leaving home to work in another country?
- What would people find unusual about living and working in your country for a short time?

Paper 1 Part 1

! Remember that matching summary sentences is similar to matching headings. Answer the questions.

- Why should you read all the paragraphs quickly first?
- Why shouldn't you worry about the meanings of individual words?
- What should you think about as you read the summary sentences?
- What should you remember when matching summary sentences to paragraphs?
- Before making your final choice of summary sentence for each paragraph, what should you do?

Verbs and meanings

5 At least one of the verbs in these pairs appears in the text. Use the pairs in their correct form to complete sentences a and b in 1–7.

> gain/win   remain/stay   borrow/lend
> feel/believe   realise/understand
> expect/look forward to   stare/glance

1 a Could you .... me some money for lunch?
   b I'll .... some money from my sister.
2 a If you subtract two from seventeen, what .... ?
   b Please come and .... with us next week.
3 a Do you .... like going out for a meal?
   b I don't .... a word Paul says.
4 a Do you .... people who speak French?
   b I didn't .... how much French I knew.
5 a I didn't .... work experience to be fun.
   b I am .... going to London in spring.
6 a Who .... the last World Cup?
   b Students can .... a lot from travelling.
7 a It's rude to .... at people!
   b Paul .... quickly through the magazine.

6 Match verbs a–f with the speakers' words in 1–6.

a suggest   c claim   e advise
b threaten   d deny   f promise

1 I didn't say three – I said two.
2 Of course I'll bring you back a present!
3 If you don't stop criticising me, I'll never to speak to you again.
4 Let's go for a pizza!
5 You ought to take more exercise.
6 I won two prizes at school for history.

Writing skills

PART 1 FORMAL TRANSACTIONAL LETTER

1 Read the question and the letter opposite, ignoring Martin's notes. Correct any information in a–c which is false.

a Anyone can go to the student conference.

b If you wish to go to the conference, you must write a letter to the Head Teacher.

c Most of the cost of the trip will be financed by the school.

2 Read Martin's reply to the letter on page 17. Has he included all the notes he made on the letter?

Formal and informal words

3 Martin is having problems finding the right kind of formal language to use. Choose one of the words or phrases a–n to replace those underlined in his letter.

a reply
b handing it in
c could you possibly
d take place
e am looking forward to receiving
f in the near future
g participating in
h am convinced
i finally
j would like
k information
l an indication
m mentioned
n received

Asking for information

4 Sentence openers a–e can all be used to ask for information. Complete the gaps using the words below, then use the completed sentence openers to find out the information in 1–5.

let	useful	like	concerned	grateful

a I would .... to know whether ... .

b I wonder if you could .... me know which ... .

c I would be .... if you could tell me whether ... .

d It would be .... to know whether ... .

e As far as (cost) is ...., how much ... ?

1 Cost of travelling to Spain?
2 Travelling by coach or train?
3 Need packed lunch?
4 Parents allowed to accompany children?
5 Languages spoken at the conference?

Your school is organising a trip to an International Student Conference in Spain. Read the letter, on which you have made some notes, sent out to students who might be interested in attending the conference.

Dear students,

when exactly?

I am writing to inform you of an exciting event which will take place <u>next year</u>. The school has been asked to send six delegates to an International Student Conference in Spain. If you would like to attend the conference, all you have to do is write <u>an essay</u> entitled 'The Importance of International Co-operation' and <u>hand it in</u> to the school secretary.

length?

what's the deadline?

The prize for the six best entries, which will be judged by a panel of teachers and two parents, will be an expenses-paid trip to the conference, but we will be asking for <u>a small contribution</u> from the parents of the winners.

how much?

We very much <u>hope you will be interested</u> in this event and we look forward to receiving your entries.

definitely!

Yours sincerely,

G Samson

George Samson, Head Teacher

Link words

5 Read this paragraph from a letter to the Head Teacher from a parent. Rewrite the paragraph using these link words in suitable places.

finally	besides this	firstly
not only ... but also		in addition

I would like to say what an excellent idea this conference is. I am certain that most of the students will welcome the chance to attend. They will enjoy the experience and learn something useful. It will give them a chance to travel to another country. They will meet people from all over the world. May I congratulate you on encouraging students to be aware of the importance of international co-operation.

Dear Mr Samson,

I was pleased to get your letter about the competition. I would be very interested in joining in this, but I need to find out some more things about the trip.

First of all, please tell me exactly when the conference will happen next year. You also mentioned writing an essay. I want to know how long you expect this to be and what the deadline for giving it to the secretary is. One last thing, you wrote something about a contribution from the parents of the winners. Could you give me some idea of how much this might be?

I'd like to receive your answer soon so that I can begin to prepare my entry for the competition, which I'm sure will be an interesting experience for the winners.

Yours sincerely,

Martin Mouchel

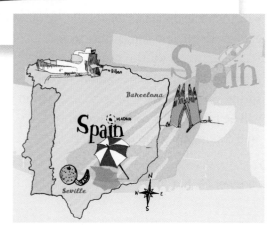

Writing checklist

All points covered/reader fully informed ☐
Well-organised layout ☐
Ideas linked clearly ☐
Appropriate style ☐
Suitable opening and closing ☐
Grammar and spelling correct ☐
The right vocabulary for the task ☐
The right length ☐
Legible handwriting ☐

Paper 2 Part 1
Correct any incorrect statements.

- The Part 1 question carries fewer marks than the Part 2 question.
- You should aim to include most of the points asked for in the question.
- It is very important to use the right tone of language.
- Use paragraphs to introduce new ideas.
- Don't bother to check your work if you are running out of time.
- It is important to know roughly how many words you write to a line.

Expressions with *take*

6 Match the expressions with *take* in a–h with meanings 1–8.

a I would like to take part in the conference.
b You should take care of yourself.
c Writing a good essay takes time.
d The success of the conference took a lot of doing.
e My new book is beginning to take shape.
f You should take advantage of any chances to travel.
g Doing physical exercise really takes it out of you.
h It's important to take it easy once in a while.

1 be hard to do
2 develop into something definite
3 look after
4 make use of or get benefit from
5 cannot be rushed
6 participate in
7 relax
8 exhaust

Writing a reply

7 Read the question in 1 again, and, using all the information in notes a–e below, write a suitable reply to the Head Teacher. Write between 120 and 180 words in an appropriate style. Use some of the sentence openers in 4 and the link words in 5. The Writing checklist will help you.

a venue – city/countryside?
b transport – plane/train?
c accommodation – hotel/host family?
d essay – hand-written/typed?
e parents' contribution – cash/cheque?

Use of English skills

PART 1 MULTIPLE-CHOICE CLOZE

1 Read the text quickly, ignoring the spaces. What environmental problem is mentioned and what is being done about it?

Silent Spring

Today is the first day of spring. It's 5.30 and the sun has not yet ⁰ .... Mist ¹ .... on the fields and the grass is wet underfoot. As the light ² .... stronger, I can ³ .... shapes: small birds singing their hearts out from rooftops and branches. But the dawn chorus is ⁴ .... more and more silent because the numbers of so many songbirds have been drastically reduced. There are many ⁵ .... for this. One is modern farming methods: fields are sprayed, fertilised and ploughed up by machines for maximum output. Hedgerows, ⁶ .... wildlife flourishes, were ⁷ .... because, at the time, no one really knew the effects of pulling them down. The result is that there is ⁸ .... for the birds to nest. So what are we going to do

⁹ .... it? Experts are ¹⁰ .... that there should be more incentives for ecologically-minded farmers, and government officials ¹¹ .... there is going to be increased funding in this area. A new seven-year plan will help and at its heart will be wildlife-friendly farming. We still ¹² .... of the countryside as being full of natural beauty, of footpaths, woods and fields. But without the proper protection, these will gradually disappear. Naturally, we all want jobs, enough to eat, and somewhere to live. ¹³ .... , we also want to hear the nightingale sing and the swallows coming home for spring. So unless we ¹⁴ .... action now, we will be putting our countryside at ¹⁵ .... and waking up to no dawn chorus.

2 For questions 1–15, read the text again and decide which answer (A, B, C or D)
CHECK best fits each space.

0 A lifted	Ⓑ risen	C climbed	D raised
1 A stretches	B extends	C lies	D covers
2 A increases	B develops	C spreads	D grows
3 A make out	B make up	C make for	D make up for
4 A changing	B becoming	C returning	D moving
5 A causes	B effects	C reasons	D purposes
6 A that	B which	C how	D where
7 A wasted	B destroyed	C extinguished	D wiped
8 A nowhere	B anywhere	C anything	D nothing
9 A for	B with	C to	D about
10 A believed	B convinced	C considered	D supposed
11 A tell	B speak	C say	D talk
12 A imagine	B think	C expect	D regard
13 A Although	B However	C Since	D Even if
14 A make	B do	C take	D hold
15 A risk	B danger	C trouble	D difficulties

TALKING ABOUT THE FUTURE

Test your knowledge

Match the future forms in bold with uses 1–9.

a I**'m going to stay in** and read a good book tonight.

b Earth's resources **will run out** in 50 years' time.

c I**'m having** a job interview on Thursday.

d I**'ll buy** you all an ice-cream when we get to the park.

e I **will pass** my driving test no matter how many times I have to take it.

f I think it**'s going to be** a nice day tomorrow.

g I**'ll have finished** this homework by lunch-time.

h **Shall I do** the washing up this evening?

i What **will we all be doing** ten years from now?

1 expressing an intention

2 talking about a definite future arrangement

3 making a promise

4 making an offer

5 making a firm prediction

6 talking about an action which will be finished before a certain future time

7 talking about an action which will be taking place at a certain future time

8 expressing determination

9 saying something may happen

3 Make sentences of your own using suitable future forms and the ideas in a–i.

a Promise to send someone a postcard.

b Say what you intend to do this weekend.

c Offer to help tidy up someone's room.

d Make a prediction about the world's wildlife.

e Say what you think the black clouds in the sky mean.

f Describe an arrangement you have made for tomorrow.

g Say what you are determined to do in the near future.

h Say when you'll have finished your homework.

i Say where you'll be spending your holidays this summer.

Exam know-how

Paper 3 Part 1

Complete the missing information.

● Before looking at questions 1–15 ....

● Even if you are sure of the answer ....

● Read each completed sentence to check that ....

Future continuous or future perfect?

4 Complete these sentences using either the future continuous (*will be doing*) or the future perfect (*will have done*).

a This time next week we (lie) on a beach in Spain.

b The family next door (move) to their new flat in the city centre tomorrow.

c We (finish) this module by the end of the week.

d My friend Lucy (come) on holiday with us this summer.

e By the end of this course I (write) ten compositions.

f Do you think you (visit) Australia when you go on your round-the-world trip?

g I hope I (pass) my exam by this time next year.

h (you/finish) your homework by 6 o'clock?

i By the year 2050, the world's population (increase) dramatically.

j This government (not bring) in any new policies in the near future.

5 Look at the time lines below and make sentences saying what you think Tim and Dave will be doing or will have done at the different times.

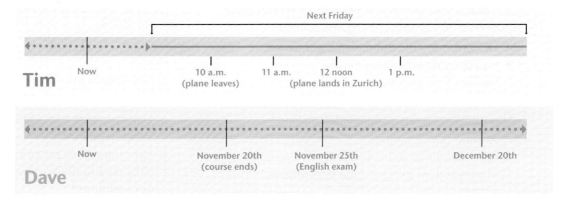

Listening skills

PART 1 MULTIPLE CHOICE
Words which sound the same

1 🎧 Listen to eight sentences from the extracts in 2 and underline the words you hear.

1	they're	there	5	we'll	wheel
2	wears	where's	6	whether	weather
3	son	sun	7	here	hear
4	course	coarse	8	been	bean

2 Read 1–8 below, then decide which pair of words a–h you might hear in which extracts.

a	entrants/promotion	e	information/download
b	cut down on/contract	f	artists/recognised
c	perfectionist/traditions	g	lifestyle/ideal
d	outlook/average	h	charter/booked

1 You hear a man and woman talking about a story in a newspaper. What was it about?

A booking a holiday to an unknown destination

B buying cheap airline tickets

C ending up at the wrong airport

2 You hear the weather forecast on the radio. What is the weather going to be like tomorrow?

A It'll be both sunny and overcast in the morning.

B There'll be heavy rain in the afternoon.

C It'll be cold for the time of year in the evening.

3 You hear a man talking to a friend about his computer. How does he feel about having one at home?

A He wastes too much time on the internet.

B He enjoys downloading music.

C He uses it occasionally for work.

4 You hear part of a radio programme about being famous. What point is the woman making?

A Anyone can be famous.

B International fame for everyone isn't possible.

C The important thing is to be remembered.

Paper 4 Part 1

Correct any incorrect statements.

- You should read all the questions before the recording starts.
- All the information on the question paper is read out.
- You don't need to understand every word you hear to answer the questions.
- You hear each extract once.

5 You hear a man talking about a cinema competition. What are the rules?

A You must write two film reviews.

B Only children can take part.

C Prizes must be used at a cinema you select.

6 You hear an advertisement on the radio. What is it for?

A protective clothing

B alarm clocks

C diving and ski equipment

7 You hear part of an interview on the radio. How has the woman's life changed recently?

A She's been spending more time with her husband.

B She's been working on a new film.

C She's been doing less travelling.

8 You hear a woman talking about her job. How does she feel about what she does?

A She wants to be as efficient as her father.

B She finds running the business easy.

C She would rather be a top chef.

3 🎧 You will hear people talking in eight different situations. For questions 1–8 in 2, choose the best answer, A, B or C. Were your predictions correct?

[CHECK]

4 Practise transferring your answers to the answer sheet in pencil, shading the correct lozenge.

Part 1						
1	A	B	C	5	A B C
2	A	B	C	6	A B C
3	A	B	C	7	A B C
4	A	B	C	8	A B C

What about you?

5 Answer these questions.

a Have you ever had a bad holiday experience? What happened?

b How important are computers in your life?

c Why do you think some people like entering competitions?

Speaking skills

PART 1 PERSONAL INFORMATION
Talking about likes, dislikes and preferences

1 Match expressions a–e with the correct prepositions, then use them (as appropriate) to say how you feel about the activities in 1–6 below.

a am (not) very fond	about
b am (not particularly) interested	on
c am (not) very keen	of
d am mad	with
e get fed up	in

2 Is this candidate's reply a good one? Why/Why not?

A *What's your favourite sport, Pedro?*

B *Well, I'm very keen on team sports, but what I really enjoy is swimming. Actually, I don't mind watching other kinds of sports on TV, but I'd rather take part in them myself.*

Exam know-how

Paper 5 Part 1
What should you do …
- if you feel nervous?
- when speaking to the examiner?
- if you don't understand what the examiner says?
- if you have no plans, interests, etc?

3 Use these expressions (as appropriate) to expand on the comments you made in 1.

Example: *I'm not keen on listening to the radio. To be honest, I find it boring.*

a To tell the truth, I love/(don't) like …
b To be honest, I find … boring/interesting.
c Actually, I can't stand …
d … bores me stiff.
e What I really enjoy is …
f As a matter of fact, I don't mind …

4 Use expressions a–d to talk about your preferences in 1–4.

a I prefer … to … .
b I'd rather (do/have) … than … .
c I like … more than … .
d I don't like … as much as … .

1 see a film/a play
2 listen to classical music/modern music
3 eat Italian food/Chinese food
4 do an outdoor job/an indoor job

5 Tell a partner what you like and dislike doing at the weekend/during the holidays/after school.

6 One word is missing in each of these sentences. Put in the missing word and read out the sentences correctly.

a I'm not particularly interested the cinema.
b I really enjoy part in sports activities.
c As a matter of fact, I don't mind listening the radio.
d What I really enjoy eating fast food.
e I prefer pop music classical music.
f I'd rather go the cinema than the theatre.
g Actually, football bores stiff.
h To tell truth, I can't stand shopping.

Revise and extend

Phrasal verbs with *take*

▶ Revision p14 Ex4

1 Match phrasal verbs a–f with meanings 1–6.

a take away
b take in
c take up
d take over
e take after
f take back

1 resemble
2 subtract
3 return
4 follow or understand
5 get control of
6 occupy (space or time)

▶ Extension p14 Ex4

2 Match the phrasal verbs in a–f with the pairs of possible meanings.

> remove/leave the ground
> adapt yourself to/form a liking for
> accept an offer/start a hobby

a William has been much fitter since he took up running last year.
b I have decided not to take up the job in Spain.
c We took off half an hour late this morning.
d Would you like to take off your coat and follow me through to the doctor's surgery?
e I didn't take to the new manager at first.
f The twins have taken to tennis like ducks to water!

3 Use phrasal verbs with *take* from 1 and 2 to complete sentences a–f.

a What time .... we .... tomorrow?
b Jane has a new boyfriend but I must admit that I didn't .... him at first.
c If you .... the child's shoes, the sales assistant can measure her feet.
d I decided to .... swimming even though I was hopeless at sports.
e Tracy has .... the idea of spending the summer working on a ranch in Australia.
f I felt that if I .... the job in the travel agency, I would enjoy it.

Words connected with work

▶ Extension p14/15 Text

4 Use the words a–h to complete sentences 1–8.

a job   c career   e staff   g promotion
b work   d salary   f qualifications h employers

1 His twenty-year .... as a government minister came to an end after the scandal.
2 I don't want a .... with responsibility.
3 Doing the garden is really hard ....
4 What kind of .... do you think you can earn as an engineer?
5 What .... do you need to be a doctor?
6 .... should always look after the interests of their workers.
7 Relationships between .... and management can sometimes be difficult.
8 The chances of .... are good if you have been with the company for more than three years.

Verbs and meanings

▶ Extension p15 Ex6

5 Use the verbs a–f in the correct form to complete sentences 1–6.

a suggest   c claim   e advise
b threaten   d deny   f promise

1 I can't understand why Paul hasn't phoned. He .... that he would call me this evening.
2 The thief .... that he had never broken into a house before.
3 The small child .... that he had broken the window playing football.
4 I .... that we go to the cinema tonight. What do you think?
5 Polly .... never to talk to me again after what I'd said about her boyfriend.
6 What do you .... me to do: leave school, or stay on and go to university?

Writing

▶ Extension p14/15

6 Write a paragraph about an experience you had which you were not looking forward to, or did not enjoy at first, but which you benefited from in some way. Say what you did, how you felt about what happened, and what you learned from the experience.

Talking about the future

▶ Revision p19

7 Put the verbs in the article below into the most suitable future form (present continuous, future continuous, *going to* (*do*), future perfect, *will*). More than one form may be possible.

Tomorrow, the government body charged with making our roads more environmentally friendly [1]....................... (meet) leading car manufacturers. In the course of their discussions, they [2]....................... (set) a target of one in ten cars to be low carbon by 2010. If we [3]....................... (improve) air quality for millions living in cities, more 'clean' cars need to be developed. Over the next few years, leading car manufacturers [4]....................... (carry) out research into new, low-emission diesel engines. It is hoped that by the end of next year, a far more efficient engine [5]....................... (designed) by these companies, and [6]....................... (be) ready for production.

▶ Extension p19

8 Decide which of the expressions, a–c, you would use to talk about an event on a timetable, and which two expressions mean *be ready to do something*. Use the phrases in their correct form to complete 1–7.

a be about to
b be on the point of
c be due to

1 We .... leaving when we realised we had lost our keys.
2 I .... leave for the airport. Can I phone you when I get back?
3 The plane .... take off at 2.30 but it was delayed by half an hour.
4 The company is doing so well that it .... take on extra staff.
5 The new motorway .... be finished next year.
6 I .... giving up my job and looking for something more challenging.
7 When .... the schools .... break up for the summer holidays?

9 Complete sentences a–g using a suitable future form of the verb in brackets and your own words.

a If we study hard, we .... (pass) ....
b I .... (get) a job .... , when I leave school.
c By the end of this term, we .... (finish) ....
d This time next week, I .... (go) ....
e I .... (meet) you for .... tomorrow.
f On Friday morning, I .... (have) an interview with ....
g This time tomorrow .... (do) my shopping.

Reading skills

PART 2 MULTIPLE CHOICE

1 Can you name these objects? What do you think they might have in common?

2 Quickly read the extract from a short story and choose the best title.

a The house in the valley

b A treasured possession

c A life of poverty

3 For questions 1–7, choose the answer (A, B, C or D) which you think fits best according to the text.

HELP

1 How did Jack get his gilt medal?

A He was given it shortly after he was born.

B His mother gave it to him when he was eleven.

C His aunt gave one to all Mrs Digby's children.

D A relative gave it to him because she liked it.

2 What does the writer mean by 'could have done with' in line 12?

A would have been better off with

B would have had no connection with

C would have got rid of

D would have taken an interest in

3 Mrs Piercy advised Jack to

A look after the medal in case of hard times ahead.

B take the medal with him wherever he went.

C hide the medal from the younger members of the family.

D treasure the medal as his own personal possession.

4 Why did Jack take the hill path one Saturday?

A He wanted to see the big house at Watching.

B He had not been able to get a lift to a nearby village.

C He decided to go for a short stroll to Hending.

D He thought he must have lost his medal there.

JACK DIGBY'S mother never gave him anything. Perhaps, as a poor woman, she had nothing to give, or perhaps she was not sure how to divide anything between the nine children. His aunt, Mrs Piercy, the
5 poulterer's wife, did give him something, a keepsake, in the form of a gilt medal. The date on it was September the 12th, 1663, which happened to be Jack's birthday, although by the time she gave it him he was eleven years old. On the back there was the figure
10 of an angel and a motto, *Desideratus* (something needed or wished for), which perhaps didn't fit the case too well, since Mrs Digby could have done with fewer, rather than more, children. However, it had taken Mrs Piercy's fancy.
15 Jack thanked her, and she advised him to stow it away safely, out of reach of the other children. Jack was amazed that she should think anywhere was out of reach of his little sisters. 'You should have had it earlier', said Mrs Piercy, 'but those were hard times.'
20 Jack told her that he was very glad to have something of which he could say, 'This is my own,' and she answered, though not with much conviction, that he mustn't set too much importance on earthly possessions.
25 He kept the medal with him always, only transferring it, as the year went by, from his summer to his winter breeches. But anything you carry about with you in your pocket you are bound to lose sooner or later. One Saturday Jack had an errand to do in Hending, but
30 there was nothing on the road that day, neither horse nor cart, no hope of cadging a lift, so after waiting for an hour or so he began to walk over by the hill path.
After about a mile the hill slopes away sharply towards Watching, which is not a village and never was,
35 only a great house standing among its outbuildings

5 What happened to Jack one frosty winter's day?

  A He discovered his medal in a small pool of water.

  B He tried unsuccessfully to recover the medal he
    had lost.

  C He found a keepsake similar to his own in the ice.

  D He broke his hand on the ice on a pond.

6 What does 'it' refer to in line 69?

  A the hill path

  B the hole

  C the earthenware pipe

  D the water

almost at the bottom of the valley. Jack stopped there for a while to look down at the smoke from the chimneys and to calculate, as anyone might have done, the number of dinners that were being cooked there that day. If he dropped or lost his keepsake he 40 did not know it at the time, for as is commonly the case he didn't miss it until he reached home again. Then he went through his pockets, but the shining medal was gone and he could only repeat, 'I had it when I started out.' 45

The winter frosts began and one day Jack thought, 'I had better try going that way again.' He halted, as before, to look at the great house, and then at the ice under his feet, for all the streams and ponds were frozen on every side of him, all hard as a bone. In a 50 little hole just to the left of the path, something no bigger than a small puddle, but deep, he saw, through the transparency of the ice, the keepsake he had been given. He had nothing in his hand to break the ice. 'Well then, jump on it.' But that got him 55 nowhere. 'I'll wait until the ice has gone,' he thought. 'The season is turning, we'll get a thaw in a day or two.'

On the next Sunday, he was up there again, and made straight for the little hole, and found nothing. 60 It was empty, after that short time, of ice and even of water. And because the idea of recovering the keepsake had occupied his whole mind that day, the disappointment made him feel lost, like a stranger to the country. Then he noticed that there was an 65 earthenware pipe laid straight down the side of the hill, and that this must very likely have carried off the water from his hole, and everything in it. No mystery as to where it led. 'The stable-yards,' thought Jack. His Desideratus had been washed down there, he 70 was as sure of that now as if he'd seen it go.

41

Exam know-how

Paper 1 Part 2

● Quickly read the title and the extract for gist.

● Even if you think you know the answer, try all the options.

● Always check that all the information is correct. Underline the relevant parts of the text.

● If the stem is not a question, turn it into a question and try to find the answer before looking at the options.

● Look at the context, reading what comes before and after to work out the meaning of unknown expressions (Q2).

● Read the text before and after the word to make sure you have the right reference (Q6).

● Global questions test your understanding of the whole text (Q7).

7 What do we learn about Jack's attitude towards his medal in the extract?

  A He was rather disappointed with it.

  B He knew that one day he would lose it.

  C He realised he would never be given anything like it again.

  D He was determined to find his lost treasure.

Confusing words

4 Use one of the verbs to complete sentences a–j.

advise/warn

a What would you .... me to study for the exam?

b Did Mary .... you not to skate on the thin ice?

reach/arrive

c When you .... at the crossroads, turn left.

d If you hurry, you will .... the town before dark.

miss/lose

e Whenever I wear gloves, I seem to .... one.

f If I left home, I know I would .... my family.

drop/fall

g Please don't .... that vase – it's worth a fortune!

h Sam didn't .... off the chair – he was pushed!

went by/went through

i Paul .... his brother's pockets to see if he had borrowed his calculator.

j Some years .... before the school friends saw each other again.

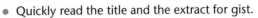
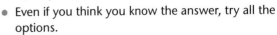

Text talk...

◆ Do you own any special objects? Why are they special?

◆ How would you feel if you lost a treasured possession?

Module 2A   25

Writing skills

1 Decide which one of these definitions best describes an article.

An article is something:
a written for an employer.
b organised under clear headings.
c written to find out information.
d written to a particular person.
e written to interest the reader.
f written to tell a story.
g written in a very formal style.

2 Read the question opposite, ignoring the article below it, then choose four of the suggested ideas in a–g below to include in your article. What order would you put them in?

a what might happen to him or her in the future
b reasons why some people don't like this star
c a physical description of the film star
d a description of his or her private life
e some of the films he or she has appeared in
f reasons why this particular film star is your favourite
g a description of the star's character

3 Now read the article and find out which of the suggested ideas in a–g in 2 the writer has included.

Linking ideas

4 Match a–f with words which mean the same in 1–6.

a although	1 during the time when
b because	2 even though
c while	3 since
d in addition	4 however
e nevertheless	5 so that
f in order to	6 moreover

5 Read the article again and choose the best link words for 1–8.

> You have been asked to write an article about your favourite film star for a magazine for film-goers. Write your answer in 120–180 words in an appropriate style.

MY FAVOURITE ACTOR

Writing checklist

All points covered/reader fully informed	☐
Well-organised layout	☐
Ideas linked clearly	☐
Appropriate style	☐
Suitable opening and closing	☐
Grammar and spelling correct	☐
The right vocabulary for the task	☐
The right length	☐
Legible handwriting	☐

I want to tell you about my favourite actor who is called Johnny Depp.

(1) Although/However/If he is in his 40s, he is handsome and charming and is physically very fit. (2) While/In addition/Nevertheless, he has a reputation for being a very good actor and working very hard on the film set.

(3) Later/After/Soon appearing in *Edward Scissorhands*, he became a well-known film star. (4) Since/After/During then, he has played many different parts in all kinds of films. He is now one of the most recognisable actors in the world.

He has acted in almost thirty feature films (5) but/as/and he has appeared in some of the best box-office successes which have ever been made. One of those films was *Once Upon A Time in Mexico*.

So why do I like him? Well, I like this actor (6) in order to/while/because he seems to be an interesting and approachable kind of man (7) despite/in spite/even if his very successful film career. Some film actors think that they are very important people (8) and/but/so not Johnny Depp. He considers himself to be a lucky man who just happens to be a film star.

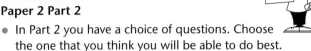
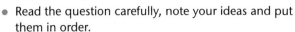
Paper 2 Part 2

- In Part 2 you have a choice of questions. Choose the one that you think you will be able to do best.
- Read the question carefully, note your ideas and put them in order.
- Write three or four paragraphs.
- Join your ideas with suitable link words.
- Use a semi-formal style.
- Make your article interesting and informative.

6 Use one of the words in 4 to complete sentences a–f.

a The film is quite old. .... , it is exciting in parts.

b We came to London .... improve our English.

c .... we were watching the film, the TV screen suddenly went blank.

d This actor has appeared in many films. .... , he has done a lot of work in the theatre.

e I like James Bond films .... they have terrific stunts.

f .... I don't watch much TV, I do enjoy watching soap operas.

despite/in spite/although

7 Complete sentences a–j using *despite*, *in spite*, or *although*.

a .... the film was long, it was very interesting.

b .... the length of the cinema queue, we didn't have to wait too long to get in.

c We enjoyed the film .... the rather poor acting.

d .... there were some big names in the film, the story was boring.

e .... of queuing for half an hour, we were unable to get a ticket for the film.

f We weren't able to get a taxi home, ... waiting for an hour in the rain last night!

g Richard managed to get the job .... not having the right qualifications.

h I wouldn't like to live in a big city .... I would enjoy all the facilities it has to offer.

i .... I don't know Tony very well, I like him.

j I enjoy living in England, ... of the awful weather!

Writing an article

8 Using the ideas and vocabulary in this section, write an article of between 120 and 180 words describing your favourite film star and saying why you like him or her. The Writing checklist on page 26 will help you.

Use of English skills

USING PRESENT TENSES

Choose the correct tense of the verb in these sentences.

a I *believe/am believing* that every country should have its own language.
b The sun *always sets/is always setting* in the west.
c What *do you think/are you thinking* about now?
d The children *play/are playing* football now.
e The new term *begins/is beginning* tomorrow.
f Interest rates *fall/are falling*.
g I *meet/I'm meeting* the new director tomorrow.

Present simple and present continuous

1 Match the examples of the present simple and present continuous in a–f with the uses in 1–6.

a Peter is revising for his exams.
b The school term starts on 6th September.
c My mother drives to work.
d The sun rises in the east.
e My younger sister is always borrowing my clothes.
f It is becoming more and more expensive to rent a flat nowadays.

1 This happens regularly.
2 This is a scientific fact.
3 This is an event on a timetable.
4 This is happening at the moment.
5 This implies that something is slowly changing.
6 This happens on a regular basis and is annoying.

Using adverbs

2 Complete sentences a–e so that they are true for you. Use the adverb in brackets in the correct position in the sentences you have made.

a I get up .... in the morning. (sometimes)
b I drink .... and eat .... for breakfast. (generally)
c I get home about .... after school. (always)
d I forget to .... when I leave the house. (never)
e I .... at the weekends. (hardly ever)

3 Decide which of the adverbs in 2 can be used at the beginning of the sentences. Where would you put the adverb *always* in these sentences?

a My friends are ringing me up about the homework.
b She is late for school.

Present simple or continuous?

4 Say which of verbs a–r can be used in the continuous form, then use some of them in the present simple or continuous to complete sentences 1–10.

a believe   g leave   m remember
b cry   h mean   n seem
c hate   i own   o smell
d forget   j prefer   p understand
e know   k read   q want
f like   l rise   r work

1 My brother .... in a fast food restaurant for a few weeks.
2 The cost of living .... at an alarming rate.
3 I .... spending some happy holidays by the sea as a child.
4 If there's one thing I .... , it's hot food that's gone cold.
5 Why .... you .... school early today?
6 .... you .... white or black coffee?
7 I .... a very interesting travel book at the moment.
8 How many students .... a mobile phone?
9 These roses .... great. Where are they from?
10 It .... as if it's stopped raining at last!

5 Use the verbs in brackets in the present simple or continuous to complete sentences a–l.

a What .... (you/eat)? It .... (smell) terrible!
b Sally's father .... (work) for a computer company in town. He's been there for years.
c What .... (your brother/do) at the moment?
d Local officials .... (try) to improve the look of the town centre.
e It always .... (rain) in May.
f .... (you/know) the answer to this question?
g It .... (appear) that they are going to build a new supermarket on the outskirts of town.
h Where .... (you/usually/do) your shopping at the weekend?
i Jacky .... (study) mathematics at university.
j What time .... you (generally/get up) in the morning?
k The half term holiday .... (begin) on Friday 14th.
l Mario and Helen .... (have) dinner together tomorrow.

The correct form of the present

6 Put the verbs in brackets in a–f into the correct form of the present, simple or continuous, active or passive.

a We .... (study) Spanish in class this year.

b To keep a record of the language, words .... (write) down and .... (transfer) to a computer.

c Four or five families in the village .... (speak) a different language.

d Our literature .... (contain) many beautiful poems.

e Chinese .... (say) to be a difficult language.

f At this very moment, children all over the world .... (teach) different languages.

PART 2 OPEN CLOZE

7 Read the text below quickly, ignoring the gaps, and find out how many languages there are in the world. How many are spoken by more than 100 million people?

Exam know-how

Paper 3 Part 2

- Quickly read the title and the text for gist.
- Read the text again, one sentence (not line) at a time.
- The sentence before or after may help you find the missing word.
- The missing word must fit grammatically and make sense in the context.
- Wrongly spelt words will not get a mark.
- Don't worry about using capital letters.
- Check your completed text by reading for overall sense.

8 For questions 1–15, read the text again and think of the word which best fits each space. Use only one word in each space.

HELP

Languages in danger

It appears that 90% of the world's languages are likely to disappear in the next half century, 0 _according_ to research conducted recently. 1 .... such language is Tofa, which is spoken by only about 60 people who herd reindeer on empty lands in central Siberia. The language 2 .... also spoken by Manchester University's Gregory Anderson, who is fluent enough to be 3 .... to express what he wants to say. Academics from the university linguistics department are holding an endangered languages day tomorrow. They 4 .... play tapes and videos of native speakers and talk about 5 .... own research and field trips all round the globe to investigate languages ranging 6 .... Faroese (50,000 speakers) to Banawa, one of 300 languages spoken in the Amazon basin. There is 7 .... shortage of languages in the world: at the last count, 8 .... were about 6,000 – but 4% of them are spoken by 96% of the people. Ten languages, 9 .... English, Arabic and Hindi, are spoken by well 10 .... excess of 100 million people each, so there is little need to worry 11 .... their future. On the other 12 .... , the minority languages with a slim chance of survival need help. A language only survives if 13 .... can be transmitted from parents to children. Every language is the storehouse of the culture of the people 14 .... speak it. As 15 .... as the last speaker is lost, the people's cultural memory is gone for ever.

Listening skills

PART 2 SENTENCE COMPLETION
Improving your spelling

1 🎧 Listen to some words and phrases and write them below. If you don't know how to spell them, guess.

a ....
b ....
c ....
d ....
e ....
f ....
g ....
h ....
i ....
j ....
k ....
l ....

2 Read sentences 1–10 in the listening task below and decide what part of speech is needed to complete them.

Exam know-how

Paper 4 Part 2
- Read the title and questions to help predict what the missing information might be.
- Only short answers are needed, so do not write too many words.
- Check that your answers fit the sentence grammatically.
- On the second listening, check that your answers make sense in the context.
- Spelling must be correct when a word is spelt out.

3 🎧 Listen to the recording and try to pencil in the right answers.
HELP

4 🎧 Listen again to check the answers you have written and to complete those you have not. What parts of speech are most of the correct answers – nouns, adjectives or verbs?

What about you?

5 Answer these questions.

a Would you be tempted to go whale-watching? Why/Why not?
b Why do you think such tours have become so popular?

You will hear radio presenter Sally Green interviewing Karl Gregson, a travel agent who organises 'whale-watching' holidays. For questions 1–10, complete the sentences.

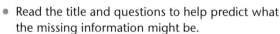
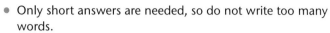

Whale-watching
a different kind of tourist activity

The experience of whale-watching can make people 1 .... , dance and sing.

It is the amazing 2 .... of the whales which makes them unusual.

Almost 3 .... a day take part in whale-watching.

Because of their 4 .... , whales are more exciting than other creatures.

Some people buy a 5 .... to raise the money for whale-watching.

Sally compares whale-watching to a 6 .... trip.

Karl suggests that using fewer 7 .... would limit the number of whale-watchers.

The aim of the tour operators is to give tourists 8 ....

Whale-watching also provides 9 .... for local people.

The whale-watching society is at 17 Green Street in 10 ....

Speaking skills

PART 2 THE LONG TURN
Explaining what you mean

1 Use the sentence openers to explain the meanings of the pairs of words a–e below.
  - That's a place where ... .
  - They're people who ... .
  - This one means ... and the other one means ... .

  a friendship/relationship
  b elderly people/grandparents
  c disco/café
  d youngsters/teenagers
  e friends/relatives

2 Match the sentences you made in 1 with the four photographs. Decide which tense you would use to describe the situations in the photographs.

3 In pairs, take it in turns to compare and contrast HELP one pair of photographs, and say how important you think the relationships are to the people. Use the words in 1, describing verbs in the present continuous, and the verbs below in the present simple.

> think   seem   look like/as if
> appear to be   imagine

4 There is at least one mistake in each of these sentences about the photographs. Find and correct them.
  a The friendship is very important for young people.
  b The elderly people look like happy.
  c The teenagers are enjoy themselves more than the elderly people.
  d These friends seem to get well with each other.
  e This person look very happy.
  f This relationship seems more closer than the one in the second picture.
  g I don't think these people are as close than the ones in the first picture.
  h Everybody likes to spend a time with their friends.
  i We must to look after elderly people.
  j The men sit in a café.

Exam know-how

Paper 5 Part 2
  - Use appropriate tenses when doing the task.
  - Don't apologise if you don't know or can't remember a word – just paraphrase.
  - Don't wait too long before you start speaking.
  - Use your imagination to make full use of the minute in your long turn.
  - Compare and contrast both photographs – don't simply describe them.

Revise and extend

Confusing words

▶ Revision p25 Ex4

1 Use these pairs of words in the correct form to complete sentences a–h.

> advise/warn   reach/arrive   miss/lose   drop/fall

a We'll .... the bus if we don't hurry.

b Oh no! I think I've .... my keys.

c When we .... at the theatre, we'll order some drinks for the interval.

d How long did it take you to .... home last night?

e My mother .... me to have a break from my homework and go for a walk.

f I think you should .... James that cycling in the middle of the road is dangerous.

g Susan .... off her bike yesterday and broke her wrist.

h I'm afraid I've .... a glass on the floor!

Phrasal verbs with *go*

▶ Extension p24/25 Text

2 Match verbs a–f with the phrasal verbs in 1–6.

a go bad   d take part in
b pass   e look carefully at
c become ill with f continue

1 Time goes by more quickly as you get older.
2 Let's go through the most important points again.
3 Sam has gone down with a bad cold.
4 Do you go in for much sport?
5 I think this milk has gone off!
6 Please go on with what you were saying.

3 Use one of the phrasal verbs in 2 in the correct form to complete these sentences.

a I think my sister's .... with 'flu.

b Don't let me interrupt you. .... with your conversation.

c I .... (not) a lot of physical exercise.

d Could you .... the grammar again before the test tomorrow?

e I can't believe how quickly time .... when you're enjoying yourself.

f Don't eat those eggs. I think they have ....

Adjectives expressing feelings

▶ Extension p24/25 Text

4 Divide these adjectives into three groups:

a positive   b negative   c positive or negative

> | amazed | disappointed | glad | upset |
> | surprised | delighted | angry | bored |
> | impatient | curious | amused | excited |

5 Match some of the adjectives in 4 with situations a–f that might make you experience these feelings.

a winning a competition
b studying a subject you aren't interested in
c wanting to find out what has happened
d finding something funny
e having an argument with a friend
f looking forward to a special treat

had better (not)

▶ Extension p24/25 Text

6 *You had better do your homework now* means *You ought to do your homework now*. Make sentences using *had better (not)* to give advice for situations a–e.

a I don't feel well.
b I forgot to tell my parents that I would be late.
c My friend Jim wants to travel round the world but he hasn't got any money.
d I can't swim.
e I'm allergic to tomatoes.

bound to/likely (to)

▶ Extension p24/25 Text

7 Say which of the phrases means

a something is certain to happen.

b there is a very good chance something will happen.

Use *bound* or *likely* and *win, pass, rain, be* or *come* to complete sentences 1–5.

1 It's .... to .... if we go for a walk. It always does.

2 Pat's .... to .... the exam because she's studied so hard.

3 Ted's .... to .... up to town next week, isn't he?

4 They say our team will .... the next world cup but I don't think it's very ...., do you?

5 William's .... to .... late. He's never on time for anything.

Expressions with *do*

▶ Extension p24/25 Text

8 What does *could have done with* mean? Underline the verbs with *do* in a–c and match them with meanings 1–3.

a We'll have to do without a holiday this year. We just can't afford one.

b In many countries they have done away with military service.

c A person's intelligence has nothing to do with how hard they work.

1 end

2 has no connection with

3 manage without having

9 Use one of the verbs in 8 in the correct form to complete sentences a–h.

a I'm sure that the robbery .... the new neighbours who moved in last week.

b The government say that they are going to .... charges for medicines.

c After I'd waited almost an hour for a bus, I could have .... a cup of coffee.

d We had to .... a car when we lived in London. We just couldn't afford one.

e Surely having a sense of humour .... being intelligent!

f It's easy to travel in European Union countries, because they .... border checks.

g There's no milk in the fridge, so you'll just have to .... it!

h I could .... more time for studying.

Writing

▶ Extension p24/25

10 You have lost something which means a lot to you. Write a notice to put on your school notice board saying:

● what you have lost.

● where and when you lost it.

● why it is important that you find it.

Include any other information you think you would need to add.

Present simple or continuous?

▶ Revision p28/29

11 Use of these verbs in the correct tense to complete 1–14.

come	call	study	remember	(not) mean
explain	stay	(not) need	have	hate
believe	enjoy	(not) speak	(not) understand	

My son normally [1] .... learning languages but at the moment he [2] .... a great time learning Japanese. A Japanese student [3] .... with us for a few months and he [4] .... teaching people his own language, so we [5] .... (all) .... Japanese with him. Sometimes I [6] .... what 'Tommy' (that's what we [7] .... him here) says, but he very kindly [8] .... it in English. I [9] .... learning Russian when I was at school and I found it difficult. I [10] .... that even if people [11] .... to learn another language, they should try to learn one. It doesn't really matter if they [12] .... it very well, at least they have tried. We all [13] .... from different places but that [14] .... that we cannot get on well with one another.

Infinitive forms

▶ Extension p29 Ex6

12 Use one of these verbs in the correct infinitive form, e.g. *to do/to be done/to be doing*, to complete sentences a–h. More than one form may be correct.

call	be	preserve	play
rise	say	live	finish

a All the world's languages ought ....

b We are lucky .... in such an exciting city.

c I would like this work .... by tomorrow.

d It's impossible .... what will happen to all the languages in the world in the future.

e Remember .... me when you get to the airport.

f Do you know how .... the guitar?

g English is said .... a difficult language to learn.

h The price of petrol appears .... again.

Reading skills

PART 2 MULTIPLE CHOICE

1 Match the adjectives below with the words in the box to describe the weather conditions in the pictures. Now quickly read the text opposite to check your answers.

| fluffy | heavy | fine | strong | thick |

(drizzle | rain | fog | wind | clouds)

2 For questions 1–8, choose the answer (A, B, C or D)

CHECK which you think fits best according to the text.

1 What problem did the writer have initially?

A He didn't hear his alarm go off.

B He found it difficult to get out of bed.

C He couldn't find the key to his room.

D He wasn't able to get out of the hotel.

2 What does 'It' refer to in line 14?

A the clock   C the hook

B the torch   D the key

3 The writer began the first part of his journey up the mountain by

A climbing very gently.

B strolling quite quickly.

C walking slowly with heavy steps.

D moving almost effortlessly.

4 The writer was taken by surprise when he

A came across an unknown creature.

B saw something move in the undergrowth.

C realised he was about to be attacked.

D heard something coming along the road.

5 Why did the writer begin to feel happier?

A The weather had started to improve.

B The road he was walking on was now less steep.

C There were no other travellers to disturb him.

D He was not in physical pain any more.

6 Where did the writer eventually decide to stop and rest for a while?

A beside a rock face

B in a chalet

C outside a ski-lodge

D in a car park

7 What does the writer mean by 'the slack period' in line 55?

A a peaceful few weeks of year

B a few moments of peace and quiet

C a boring interval between jobs

D a quiet time for business

Alpine adventure

My watch alarm woke me at five. I lay still, listening for rain. There it was again, out in the darkness, challenging me to stay in bed. But the day ahead was going to be long and strenuous and so I flung off the duvet, packed and crept downstairs. The front door was locked and I fumbled behind the desk for a key. 5
I found a jangling jailer's bunch but none fitted. Using my torch I tiptoed through the kitchen but the rear exit was also locked. A clock chimed the half hour.

I sat down, wondering whether it would be wise to wake the manageress at 5.30 a.m., but where was she? In the 10 restaurant the trout tank bubbled while above my head the clock ticked away the precious seconds. I shone my torch round the reception area. Something glinted: a solitary brass key on a hook. It worked, and like an escaping prisoner I reached the wet pre-dawn street without setting off an alarm. 15

The steep road did not allow me to begin the day gently. But, well-practised in mountain walking, I set off at a steady plod past silhouettes of cuckoo clock houses and farms perched above the U-shaped bends in the road. The heavy rain turned to fine drizzle and dim light 20 filtered into the valley. The fluffy clouds turned purple, mauve, then pink, and I could see the river valley stretching away to the east and west, the cattle in its meadows as still as haystacks as they waited for their later dawn. 25 The drizzle ceased and I stopped at a cold clear stream to drink, and sat watching a faint rainbow forming in the west.

I was about to set off again when a sudden movement prompted me 30 to stop. At first I thought it might be a squirrel but

8 What do we learn about the writer in the extract?

  A He disliked being out of doors in bad weather.

  B He made the best of the difficulties he encountered.

  C His aim was to reach the top of the Jura mountains.

  D He hadn't done any serious mountain walking before.

the creature which bounded across the road was far too big. It was as large as a domestic cat. I froze. It spotted me, but

35 instead of disappearing into the undergrowth, it leapt effortlessly on to a beech log and crouched there as though posing for a wildlife photograph. It stared at me with inquisitive black eyes, then, more bored than afraid, glided noiselessly into the wild wood.

40 The road continued to rise at a steady angle. No vehicles passed me and the only sounds were of water, the strong wind blowing, and birdsong. My legs no longer ached and my leather boots, stretched by the rain, now fitted my feet. At last I was beginning to enjoy myself, and singing, I

45 gradually gained altitude. I was eager to see the pass from which I would be able to see the Jura mountains. But towards the top my hopes were dashed by fog so thick that a false night seemed to have fallen around me.

A rock face became a building; a monstrous ski-lodge, its

50 locked doors and shuttered windows showing no lights. The chill was so intense that I continued up the road with my teeth chattering. Where was the top? The fog was so thick that I almost missed a dim light glowing from a chalet which, on closer inspection, turned out to be a cafeteria.

55 The owner was using the slack period between seasons to varnish a pine wall while his wife fed their blond toddler. 'Is this the summit?' I asked, and it was. The windows rattled and the smoky fog persisted, but it was only 8.30 and I

60 lingered, hoping the sun might dissolve the gloom and present me with a vision of Switzerland. But after four coffees, I set off again into the murk. At least it was all

65 downhill now, and I walked quickly, anxious to rejoin the visible world again.

Text talk...

* Why do you think some people enjoy mountain walking so much?

* What would it be like to live and work in a place which people only visit in the tourist season?

Paper 1 Part 2

Correct any incorrect advice.

* Work through the multiple-choice questions as you read the extract for the first time.

* Cross out the parts of the text which do not contain answers to the questions.

* If you don't know an expression, work out its meaning from the context.

* If the stem is a question, turn it into a statement.

* If you think you know the answer, don't bother reading the other options.

* For questions about reference words, read what comes before and after the word.

* The answer to global questions is based on the text as a whole.

Body movements

3 Decide whether verbs a–h from the extract are used to talk about the writer or the creature on the mountain, then match them with meanings 1–8.
What are the past forms of a–h?

a fling	c fumble	e bound	g crouch
b creep	d tiptoe	f leap	h stare

1 look for a long time with eyes wide open
2 move forwards with jumping movements
3 handle awkwardly
4 rest near the ground with bent knees
5 throw something violently
6 walk with heels raised off the ground
7 jump high or a long way
8 move slowly, quietly and carefully

Phrasal verbs with *set*

4 Replace the underlined words in a–e with phrasal verbs made from *set*. Two of the verbs can be used with a similar meaning.

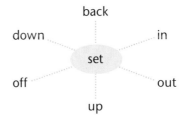

a We <u>left</u> on the first stage of our journey in January.
b The bad weather <u>delayed the progress of</u> the expedition by three days.
c <u>Write</u> your ideas on this piece of paper.
d The company was <u>established</u> about ten years ago.
e Bad weather has <u>started and is likely to continue</u>.

Writing skills

PART 2 ARTICLE BASED ON A SET BOOK

1 Mario has read a book of short stories called *Ghost Stories*. Read the extract opposite from one of the stories and answer these questions.

a Where was Giles?
b Why was it difficult for Giles to see clearly?
c What might have saved Giles's life?
d Who had shown Giles the route?
e What do you think happened next?

2 From the choice of two questions, Mario has decided to answer exam question (a) below. He needs to write 120 to 180 words. From the list a–g, choose three main points which you think he will concentrate on in his article.

a the writer's personality
b what happens to the characters in the story
c the historical period the book is set in
d how the reader gets involved in the story
e how the story ends
f why the story is so exciting
g the kind of language the writer uses

> (a) 'This is such an exciting story that you will not be able to put it down.' Write an **article** for your class magazine, saying whether you agree with this statement or not with reference to the book or one of the short stories you have read.

The Stranger in the Mist

Giles walked fast. The mist had become thicker than before, but the path was a good one. From time to time he checked his route on the map. Soon the path led him down a very steep hillside. In the mist, Giles could see only a few feet ahead, so he moved very carefully. Suddenly his foot turned on a sharp stone and he almost fell. That stone probably saved his life. It flew up from under his feet and rolled down the steep path. He heard it rolling faster and faster, then the noise stopped. A few seconds later Giles heard a crash as the stone hit the ground hundreds of feet below. The path had led him to the edge of a cliff! Giles picked up another stone and dropped it. Again he heard the distant crash as it fell over the cliff. He looked at the map again. There was no cliff on the route that the old man had shown him. For the first time, Giles became seriously worried. He sat down miserably on a large rock, took out his pipe, and found a match to light it. 'Well', he thought, 'I'll just have to sit and wait for the mist to clear.'

3 Read Mario's article, ignoring gaps 1–10. Were your predictions in 2 correct? Which two verbs in paragraphs 2 and 3 would be better in the past perfect?

5a GHOST STORIES
Oxford Bookworms Collection

<u>Read this if you dare!</u>

¹............ I enjoyed all the short stories, the most exciting was *The Stranger in the Mist*. It is about a man called Giles ²............ went to Wales on holiday. Giles was interested in geology, and one day he went walking in the mountains but got lost in the mist.

An old man with his dog gave Giles a map ³............ he could find his way back home. ⁴............, as you read, you slowly realise that the man gave Giles a very old map ⁵............ no longer showed the real path.

The story is exciting ⁶............ you want to know who the man was, and, ⁷............, you cannot put the book down. You imagine that you are lost like Giles. You think that you have met a helpful old man, ⁸............, the next minute, you nearly fall over an enormous cliff. You are afraid, ⁹............ he was, ¹⁰............ he realised that he nearly died on the mountain. You want to get to the bottom of the mystery so you read on.

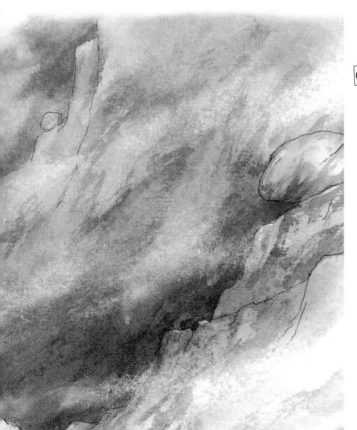

Paper 2 Part 2

Match the sentence halves.

a Read both questions then ...	1 semi-formal style.
b Make a list of points then ...	2 choose the one you think you can do best.
c Divide your article into ...	3 make your article interesting and informative.
d Join your ideas with ...	4 three or four paragraphs.
e Use a ...	5 suitable link words.
f Remember your audience and ...	6 decide which order you will put them in.

Link words

4 Use these link words to complete 1–10 in Mario's article.

> when   which   as   so that   because   then
> for that reason   although   who   however

Expressions with *bottom*

5 What does the expression *get to the bottom of* mean in Mario's article ? Underline the expressions with *bottom* in a–d, then match them with meanings 1–4.

a We cleaned the house from top to bottom.
b Sam started at the bottom of his profession.
c Our football team came bottom of the league last year.
d The bottom has fallen out of the second-hand car market.

1 in the last position   3 completely
2 trade has collapsed in   4 in the lowest position

Writing about a story

6 Using the ideas and vocabulary in this section, write an article of between 120 and 180 words about an exciting story you have read. The Writing checklist will help you.

Writing checklist

All points covered/reader fully informed	☐
Well-organised layout	☐
Ideas linked clearly	☐
Appropriate style	☐
Suitable opening and closing	☐
Grammar and spelling correct	☐
The right vocabulary for the task	☐
The right length	☐
Legible handwriting	☐

Use of English skills

TALKING ABOUT PAST EXPERIENCES

Test your knowledge

Correct any mistakes you find in these sentences.

a Suddenly, the skies became dark and the wind started howling.
b I was walking along the waterfront when I was seeing someone I knew.
c What did you do when you visited Florence?
d Who was this guidebook wrote by?
e I was working as a secretary and my husband was writing a book.

Uses of the past simple and past continuous

1 Match the uses of the past simple and the past continuous with sentences 1–6.

a a series of actions in the past
b a regular past occurrence which no longer happens
c a past situation that existed over a period of time
d two actions happening together in the past
e an action going on when another occurred
f a single action in the past

1 I travelled to work by train yesterday morning.
2 As a student, I spent several months in Italy.
3 I used to go to the theatre every week.
4 I got up early, had breakfast and caught the train.
5 I was driving to work when I heard the news.
6 We were having coffee in the garden and the children were playing nearby.

Past simple or past continuous?

2 Use these verbs in the correct form to complete 1–11.

spot	eat	set	travel	feel	aim
sleep	think	wear	arrive	sit	

It was a beautiful afternoon, so we [1] .... we might try our hand at 'drifting'. Drifting is a really safe way for beginners to do a bit of white-water rafting. Everyone in the group [2] .... yellow waterproofs and life jackets. We [3] .... quickly down the river in our large rubber dinghy when we suddenly [4] .... the white, frothing rapids ahead. Somewhat alarmed, we [5] .... the dinghy straight at the centre of the churning waves and, as luck would have it, eventually [6] .... at our destination further downstream just as the sun [7] .... It [8] .... good to be on dry land again. We [9] .... a satisfying meal, then [10] .... around the camp fire watching the flames flickering. But before they had died out, everyone [11] .... soundly in their tents.

The correct past form

3 Complete 1–10 with the correct form of the verbs in brackets.

The next stop on our trip was the Ice Hotel, just outside Kiruna. The whole building [1] .... (make) out of huge blocks of ice. Guests [2] .... (drink) at the Ice Bar as we [3] .... (go) into the gigantic igloo. We [4] .... (give) special sleeping bags by the friendly staff, and ice beds which [5] .... (cover) in reindeer skins. We [6] .... (sleep) very well given the circumstances but we quickly [7] .... (come) to the conclusion that one night was enough. The next day, we [8] .... (take) to a cosy forest chalet, where we [9] .... (gaze) at the northern lights, watching them flicker and glow through windows in the roof. Our final visit was to the Ice Hotel Art Centre, where we [10] .... (invite) to admire the ice sculptures.

Past simple and past continuous passive

4 Rewrite sentences a–d using the sentence openers given.

a The guide handed the receptionist the guests' passports.
The guests' passports ....
The receptionist ....

b They were showing the passengers a film on board the boat.
A film ....
The passengers ....

c The passengers gave the guide a tip at the end of the voyage.
The guide ....
A tip ....

d They were giving the passengers questionnaires about the voyage to fill in.
Questionnaires ....
The passengers ....

Exam know-how

Paper 3 Part 2
Complete the missing information.

● Before you answer the questions, quickly ....
● Read the text again, one .... (not line) at a time.
● The sentence .... or .... may help you find the missing word.
● The word must fit .... and ....
● You will lose marks for ....
● You will not lose marks for ....
● Check your answers by ....

CHECK

PART 2 OPEN CLOZE

5 Read the text below quickly, ignoring the spaces, and find out who the writer met.

6 For questions 1–15, read the text again and think of the word which best fits each space. Use only one word in each space.

CHECK

the beauty of SWEDEN

I never used to be interested in visiting northern countries but Sweden changed my attitude. The best thing to do when you first arrive in Stockholm **0** *is* take a stroll around the magnificent harbour. The weekend I visited, **1** .... kind of seafaring vessel had put into port, **2** .... Viking ships to international cruise liners. The water **3** .... dotted with weekend sailboats and the quayside was full **4** .... cyclists and children fishing. We wandered along the waterfront past the Parliament building and lingered in the medieval heart of Stockholm, exploring the maze of 16th century town houses. After a weekend in the city, **5** .... was time to board a train and head north to Swedish Lappland. **6** .... we were enjoying the on-board cinema and restaurant, the high-speed train Nordpilen was heading quietly for the heart of the Swedish forests. Seventeen hours **7** .... , we woke to find **8** .... in the very different world of Lappland. **9** .... you want to know what winter's really **10** .... , this is the place to come. I was taken to meet Wilhelm Seva, a 55-year-old reindeer herder **11** .... was happy to recall his childhood spent in the forest. 'Now it's snowmobiles and warm houses in winter for most of us, but **12** .... are still a few herders who spend all year in the forest, as I used **13** .... ,' he says. Another local told **14** .... about the new Arctic snowmobile trail he'd just tested. 'Why **15** .... try it next time?' he laughed. 'It's only 3,000km long and goes in a loop through the whole of Lappland!'

Listening skills

PART 2 SENTENCE COMPLETION

1 Read the information in task 2 below. Which sentences in 1–10 do you think answer questions a–j about 'builderers'?

   a What's the difference between a rock climber and a 'builderer'?
   b What should you obtain before the climb?
   c What do 'builderers' manage without?
   d How can you advertise your climb?
   e Why do climbers do this activity?
   f What do you need a good supply of?
   g What kind of buildings are not challenging to climb?
   h Who is likely to become a 'builderer'?
   i What did one 'builderer' end up doing?
   j When should you do your climb?

2 🎧 You will hear Robert Harding, a journalist, talking about 'builderers', people who climb high buildings for fun. For questions 1–10, complete the sentences.

CHECK

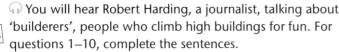

A different kind of leisure activity

Anyone ¹ .... about climbing will want to be a 'builderer'.

The need for ² .... makes climbers become 'builderers'.

Never climb a building without getting ³ .... first.

'Builderers' do not generally use ⁴ ....when they climb.

A good time for a climb is a ⁵ ....

The best way to get publicity for a climb is to invite ⁶ ....

You must take plenty of ⁷ .... to help you climb the building.

Unlike a rock climber, a 'builderer' looks for the ⁸ ....

Surprisingly enough, ⁹ .... buildings are easy to climb.

One French climber became a professional ¹⁰ ....

Words in context

3 Which answers in a–f do you think would be correct? Why?

   a 'Builderers' are _real life/relive_ Spider-Men.
   b 'Buildering' is not safe for an _amateur/animator_ climber.
   c Climbers like buildings that look like a _rock face/rough place_ .
   d Professional climbers are not afraid of _hits/heights_ .
   e Choose a time when there is not much _terrific/traffic_ in the area.
   f Platforms used by _winter cleanings/window cleaners_ help 'builderers'.

Exam know-how

Paper 4 Part 2
Complete the advice.

- Use the time allowed for reading the text to ....
- Write only ....
- Always check the words you have written are .... and fit in ....
- Use the second listening to check that your answers ....
- If a word is spelt out make sure ....

What about you?

4 Answer these questions.

   a Why do you think people enjoy climbing high buildings?
   b Should people who take risks expect others to rescue them when things go wrong? Why/Why not?

Speaking skills

PART 2 THE LONG TURN

1 If you were given these two photographs in the exam, what do you think the examiner would ask you to do?

2 Compare the task on page 115 with your idea in 1.

3 🎧 Listen to two candidates do the task in 2, or read it on page 115. Tick which of the following each candidate does. Which candidate deals with the task successfully?

	First cand.	Second cand.
a Describe each photo individually.	☐	☐
b Compare what is happening in both photos.	☐	☐
c Repeat the same thing.	☐	☐
d Make a lot of grammatical mistakes.	☐	☐
e Paraphrase a word.	☐	☐
f Link his/her ideas about both photos.	☐	☐
g Stop talking too early.	☐	☐
h Talk for about a minute.	☐	☐

Using comparatives and superlatives

4 Complete sentences a–e using a comparative or superlative form, e.g. *more ... than, as ... as, most*.

a The man in the first photo looks .... (worry) .... the man in the second photo.

b This man doesn't seem to be in .... much of a hurry .... the man in the second photo.

c I think the second man will be in .... trouble .... the first man if he is late.

d It's difficult to say who is in the .... (big) .... hurry.

e The .... important thing is that they both arrive on time.

Exam know-how

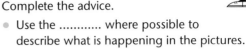

Paper 5 Part 2

Complete the advice.

● Use the .... where possible to describe what is happening in the pictures.

● If you cannot think of a word, ...

● You will need to use .... if you find you have little to say.

● It is not enough simply to .... one picture, then the other.

5 Do the tasks below in pairs. CHECK

Task 1

Student A: Read out the task on page 117 to your partner. Time your partner and stop him/her after a minute.

Student B: Look at the photos below. Listen to the task, then talk for about a minute. Stop when your partner tells you.

Task 2

Student B: Read out the task on page 118, then time your partner and stop him/her after a minute.

Student A: Look at the photos on page 116. Listen to the task, then talk for about a minute. Stop when your partner tells you.

Revise and extend

Body movements

▶ Revision p35 Ex3

1 Use one of these verbs in the correct form to complete sentences a–h. More than one answer may be correct.

fling	creep	fumble	tiptoe
bound	leap	crouch	stare

a Jim woke up early, ... off the bedclothes and ran to the window.

b It's rude to .... at people!

c If we .... along the corridor without our shoes, no one will be able to hear us!

d The small child .... down in the corner of the room and refused to come and say 'hello'.

e We .... out of the house, afraid that someone would hear us close the front door.

f Suddenly a cat .... across the road in front of us.

g Do you think we can .... across this stream without getting wet?

h Richard .... with his keys and tried to open the car door.

Words connected with travelling

▶ Extension p34/35 Text

2 Use one of these words in its correct form to complete sentences a–h.

trip	tour	voyage	journey
drive	flight	travel	ride

a The long ocean .... from Britain to Australia used to take months.

b My mother goes on a lot of business .... abroad.

c We haven't decided whether we are going to .... by train or car.

d How long does your .... to work take?

e Several airlines are now offering cut-price .... to many destinations.

f If you like horses, we could go for a .... tomorrow.

g It's worth going on a guided .... of the city if you want to see the sights.

h It's only about ten minutes' .... from here to the city centre by car.

Phrasal verbs with *turn*

▶ Extension p34/35 Text

3 Match the verbs with *turn* in sentences a–f with meanings 1–6.

a We'll have to turn back. The snow is too deep.

b You can't turn down the offer of a job like this!

c Tadpoles eventually turn into frogs.

d It turned out that we had lived next door to each other as children.

e If you turn over the page, you will see the exercise I am talking about.

f Guess who turned up at the party last night?

1 return to where we came from

2 refuse

3 look at the other side

4 become

5 appear (unexpectedly)

6 be discovered

4 Use one of the phrasal verbs with *turn* in 3 in the correct form to complete sentences a–f.

a A lot of people .... at the meeting yesterday.

b I think we'll have to .... We can't drive any further in this weather.

c Hens' eggs .... little yellow chicks.

d The weather has .... nice this morning.

e Please .... the page and read the question at the top.

f Guess what? Brian has .... that job he was offered!

Writing

▶ Extension p34/35

5 Write a postcard to a friend describing a terrible journey to your holiday destination. Say what happened and how you dealt with the problem.

used to do/would do

⟩ Extension p38 Ex1

6 Decide in which sentence either *used to* or *would* can be used. Why can *would* not be used in the other one?

a Every winter, we .... go to the mountains.

b This building .... be an old palace.

7 Use one of these verbs and either *used to* or *would* to complete sentences a–f. In which sentences is it not possible to use *would*?

| live | be | make | give | like | go |

a My grandparents .... in Australia.

b Who .... to the cinema on a Saturday morning when they were a child?

c You never .... coffee!

d The teacher .... us our homework on a Friday afternoon.

e There are far more cars on the roads than there ....

f What .... me happy was the long summer holiday.

Past simple tense

⟩ Revision p38/39

8 Write these irregular verbs in the past simple, then use an appropriate verb in the past simple (active or passive) to complete sentences a–j.

beat	become	blow	build	choose	cost
fight	freeze	grow	hear	lead	ride
read	shake	spend	steal	throw	wake

a Several trees .... down by the strong winds.

b The weather was so cold that even John's beard .... !

c I've told the police my bicycle .... last night.

d The trip to Sweden .... more than I thought it would.

e You .... these vegetables in your own garden, didn't you?

f We .... an interesting book in class last month.

g The ground .... as the fireworks exploded.

h Our local football team .... by their opponents in the match last weekend.

i Who .... that ball into the garden?

j A friend of mine .... a team of climbers on an expedition to Kilimanjaro.

Past simple, past continuous, or *used to*?

⟩ Revision p38/39

9 Complete the text with the correct form of the verbs .

Every summer when the children were small we
[1] .... (go) to the south of France on holiday.
We always [2] .... (take) the car on the motor-
rail and [3] .... (drive) back. One summer,
while we [4] .... (travel) along a particularly
beautiful stretch of road on our return journey, my
husband, who [5] .... (do) the map reading
at the time, [6] .... (decide) to take a detour,
thinking that we might see some beautiful scenery.
The children [7] .... (argue) in the back of the
car and [8] .... (need) something to distract
them. As I [9] .... (approach) we one of the
sharp bends on the hillsides, we [10] ....
(notice) that the road [11] .... (become)
narrower and narrower. After about another 20
minutes, it suddenly [12] .... (come) to an
abrupt end. It [13] .... (begin) to look as if
we [14] .... (be) all about to spend the night
sleeping in the car.

Describing pictures

⟩ Extension p41

10 Correct the mistakes in sentences a–j.

a The people in this picture don't look as happier as those in the second picture.

b The both pictures show people taking care of someone.

c These people looks really tired.

d It must be very satisfied to do a job like this.

e I think the children isn't enjoying themselves.

f This is not ordinary job. It's way of life.

g The people look happy, aren't they?

h Maybe it's most difficult to look after the children than the adults.

i I think people choosing jobs like these because they enjoy working with others.

j The girl in the picture read a book.

Reading skills

PART 3 MISSING SENTENCES

1 Name the capital city in the photo, and some of its famous landmarks, and discuss why this place has always attracted so many writers and artists.

2 Read the article, ignoring the gaps, and find out why George's home is rather different from ordinary homes.

3 Seven sentences have been removed from the article. Choose from the sentences A–H the one which fits each gap (1–6). There is one extra sentence which you do not need to use.

HELP

A He never got further than central America, but that journey shaped his life.

B There, a wooden staircase leads up to the children's section and more rooms, their ceilings cracked and blackened from the fire that almost razed the store in the 1990s.

C Once the eye adjusts to the spines, you notice the suitcases, backpacks, T-shirts and towels peeking from behind bookcases, and the visitors' sleeping bags propped in corners.

D But twice that number often roam the store, and there are rarely fewer than a dozen sleeping there.

E They describe their businesses as 'sister bookshops', though there is little in the way of family resemblance.

F The only modern items to be seen are the exposed electrical wiring and a paraffin heater in the corner, ready for another hard winter.

G In those days, George sat (in the back of the store, in a small overcrowded room, with a desk and a small stove), undernourished, bearded, lending his books to people, and housing penniless friends upstairs.

H Since then, some of the last century's greatest literary figures have passed through, to recite their work or consult the sprawling shelves of this curious 'rag-and-bone shop of the heart'.

Home is where the heart is

Over half a century ago an American expatriate opened a bookstore on the left bank of the river Seine.
[0 | H] Equal parts bookshop, library,
5 hostel and museum, *Shakespeare and Company* is a place so otherworldly it seems to exist in a time warp. It's a place where strangers are invited to 'raid the icebox, kick off your
10 shoes and lie in bed'. On its walls are pictures of George the owner, together with his oldest friend, American poet Lawrence Ferlinghetti, proprietor of another
15 great literary institution, San Francisco's *City Lights* bookstore.
[1 |] *City Lights* is a tight, professional ship. The family bond rests in their shared love of
20 literature and poetry. A combined century of bookmanship unites them: they have fed and sheltered writers and publishers of

literature and poetry, and helped
25 countless unknowns along the way.
　　The foundations of the place were laid a thousand years ago. Put up in the 16th century, the building was a monastery, and it is steeped in
30 history: twisted oak beams and crumbling plaster overhead, cracked tiles underfoot. [2 |] Although George has steadily acquired more of the building, adding rooms one
35 by one to his original ground-floor premises, little has changed since the 1950s. [3 |] Even today, all those who come for books stay on to talk, while George tries to write
40 letters, to open his mail, to order books. A tiny, unbelievable staircase, circular, leads to the bedrooms, where his guests are free to stay.
　　And everywhere, books, stacked
45 every which way, lining walls from ceiling to floor, piled on shelves and tables. [4 |] George welcomes all this, feeds his guests, puts them up for as long as they

HELP

Paper 1 Part 3

- Read the main text for gist and to identify what kind of information is missing.
- Read sentences A–H and find words which refer to something in the main text.
- Try every sentence (apart from the example) in each gap before making your final choice.
- Check the extra sentence again to make sure you do not need it.

---

50 want. He explains that he is simply repaying the kindness shown to him over 60 years ago when he set out to walk round the world.

[5 ⬚] His house will always be open to
55 writers, dreamers, students and teachers. Guests can clean, cook or work in the shop. Or not. There are few rules, other than respect for fellow guests.

Since there is no fire escape, the city
60 authorities have told George to restrict customers to fifteen at any one time.

[6 ⬚] 'One man has been living here for five years,' says George proudly. 'He came here, got some of his poetry published,
65 and now he's doing translations. He's changed his whole life.'

These life-enhancing qualities are echoed on the shop's website, where people post testimonials about life in
70 Paris, and how George introduced them to poetry, friendship and sharing, indeed to life itself.

Words connected with buildings

4 Divide these words into types of buildings and things found inside buildings, then use them to complete sentences a–j.

> ground floor   beams   plaster   monastery
> tiles   wiring   foundations   staircase
> premises   ceiling   shelves   hostel

a Be careful going up stairs – the boards on the .... are loose.
b When the business expanded, it had to move to larger ....
c We'll have to do something about that crumbling .... on the living room walls on the ....
d I think the .... on the bedroom light is faulty.
e All those books are too heavy for these ....
f There is a very cheap youth .... in the centre of town.
g The old .... fell into disuse last century when the monks moved nearer to the city centre.
h The kitchen's cold in winter because of the ceramic floor ....
i The .... of the building were laid hundreds of years ago.
j These wooden .... on the .... above the fireplace in the living room date back to the 17th century.

Phrasal verbs with *put*

5 What two meanings does *put up* have in lines 27 and 48? Match these verbs with *put* with their possible meanings a–d, then use them to complete sentences 1–4 below.

> put up with   put off   put in   put out

a extinguish
b spend time/energy doing
c tolerate or bear
d discourage

1 You will need to .... a lot more work if you want to do well in the test tomorrow.
2 I hope I haven't .... (you) .... the idea of working in a bookshop. It's quite interesting really.
3 They managed to .... the fire in the building.
4 I don't think I can .... that noise from next door any longer.

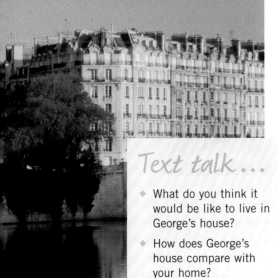

Text talk...

- What do you think it would be like to live in George's house?
- How does George's house compare with your home?

Writing skills

PART 2 REPORT

1 Underline the key words in the question opposite, then think about the meaning of *cultural holiday*. What kinds of activities might be included in a visit like this? Fill in the boxes on the mind map with your own ideas in note form, then compare your ideas with a partner's.

Some English-speaking students are visiting your area on a week's cultural holiday. The organisers have asked you to write a report suggesting what activities they might do. Write your report in 120–180 words.

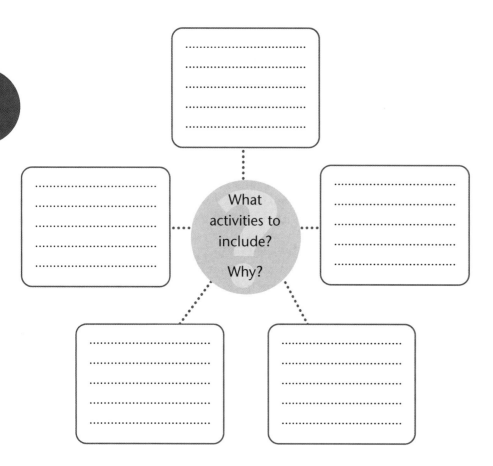

Here are four activities which I consider to be suitable for the students coming to stay in the area.

1 ....
We are lucky to have several museums in the town and I (a) .... the students to one or two of these during their stay. This will give them an idea of our towns' past and what happened here in the past.

2 Read the report opposite which Thanos has written, and match these headings to paragraphs 1–4. Ignore gaps a–d and any mistakes.

Leisure and fitness   Local history   Local specialities   Wildlife

3 Find and correct four mistakes in the report.

2 ....
Just outside the town there is a safari park.
The students (b) .... a guided
tour of the park and learn about the animals
which you can find there. The nature is
beautiful and you can have a picnic there.

3 ....
I (c) .... to the new sports centre.
The students will find all kinds of sports there
and can enjoy the open-air swimming pool if
a weather is fine.

4 ....
Finally, I (d) .... are taken to a
restaurant to try some dishes which are
characteristic of the area.

These cultural and leisure activities should
make the students' stay intresting and
enjoyable.

Writing checklist

All points covered/reader fully informed	☐
Well-organised layout	☐
Ideas linked clearly	☐
Appropriate style	☐
Suitable opening and closing	☐
Grammar and spelling correct	☐
The right vocabulary for the task	☐
The right length	☐
Legible handwriting	☐

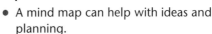

Exam know-how

Paper 2 Part 2

- A mind map can help with ideas and planning.
- Include all the information asked for.
- Use headings for each new paragraph in a report.
- Use a semi-formal style.

Making suggestions and recommendations

4 Complete gaps a–d in the report using the phrases below.

- suggest that the students
- could have
- suggest taking
- would definitely recommend going

5 Complete sentences a–e using the verbs in brackets and any other necessary words.

a I recommend that you .... (go) to the Italian restaurant.
b I would definitely recommend .... (visit) the new shopping centre.
c I suggest that you .... (take) them to the art museum.
d I suggest .... (spend) a day in the countryside.
e You .... (have) a nice picnic by the lake.

Using the passive

6 You can make a report more formal by using the passive. Turn sentences a–d into the passive and begin with either *I recommend ...* or *I suggest ...* .

a Why don't you give the students a free afternoon to explore the town?
b How about introducing the students to some of the local people?
c It's a good idea to take the students on a river trip.
d You should encourage the students to learn about our local history.

Writing a report

7 Write a report for the organisers like the one
HELP opposite, but referring to the area where you live.
Use the ideas in this section and the Writing checklist to help you.

Use of English skills

PRESENT PERFECT TENSE

Present perfect simple and continuous

1 Match the verb forms in a–e with uses 1–6.
More than one answer may be correct.

a You've torn your jacket!
b My parents have bought a house in Spain.
c I've been studying English for five years.
d This is the third time I've seen the film
   The Lord of the Rings.
e I've been waiting for you for over an hour!

1 to show we are more interested in what
   has happened than when it happened
2 to emphasise how many times an action
   happened
3 to express anger or irritation
4 to show that the action is finished but
   we can see the result
5 to emphasise the length of the action
6 to suggest that this is still true or
   happening

2 Complete sentences a–h using the
present perfect (simple or continuous).

a In my career, I (teach) students of all
   different ages.
b I (live) with my sister for the past few
   months.
c Our family (live) in three different countries.
d This is the first time Tim (play) in a
   proper band.
e What (you/do) since we last met?
f (you/ ever/write) a short story that's
   been published?
g This is the second pair of trainers (I) buy
   this year.
h I (cut) my finger. Have you got a bandage?

Past simple and present perfect with *for* and *since*

3 Explain the difference between *for* and *since* in the example
sentences below, and complete a–e with *for* or *since,* and the
present perfect (simple or continuous) or past simple.

- Eve has been studying at this school *for* six months.
- It's six months *since* we moved into this house.

a David .... (study) music .... three years before joining
   a professional band.
b I .... (play) in this orchestra ever .... my career
   .... (begin).
c We .... (stand) at this bus stop .... one o'clock and
   there is still no sign of the bus.
d 'How long .... (you/study) Greek?' '............ six months
   now.'
e Tim .... (be) a teacher .... he .... (leave)
   university.

Present perfect with *still, yet, already* and *just*

4 Rewrite sentences a–e using the words in brackets. You may need
to change other words in the sentences.

a Your mother rang to give you a message a moment ago. (just)
b The TV programme hasn't finished yet. (still)
c The students went home about 20 minutes ago. (already)
d The children are still doing their homework. (yet)
e The lesson began a few minutes ago. (just)

5 Read the text below and put the verbs in brackets in 1–8 into the
present perfect (simple or continuous).

new kid on the decks

*Giles Tremlett meets the 11-year-old
who's on the road to superstardom*

I ¹ .... (finally/track) Ben King down to a night-club in
eastern Spain. Since lunch-time, Ben ² .... (rehearse)
on the 'decks' in the empty club. Ben's energetic mum, Bev,
who ³ .... (give up) doing a law degree to run Ben's
career, has all the qualities of a showbiz mum, starting with
absolute faith in her son's talents. Ben's family ⁴ ....
(bet) everything on promoting 'DJ Kingy – Kid Sensation'. They
are so sure that he will make it in a world where top DJs can
earn as much as film stars that they ⁵ .... (move) to be

PART 3 KEY WORD TRANSFORMATIONS

6 For questions 1–10, complete the second sentence so that it has a similar meaning to the first sentence, using the word given. Do not change the word given. You must use between two and five words, including the word given.

> ❗ **Look out for (1)**
>
> - tense changes
> - *for* and *since*
> - phrasal verbs
> - fixed phrases
> - modals
> - adverbs ↔ adjectives

Example:

Ben's age is of no importance in his job as a DJ.

difference

Ben's age does *..not make any difference..* to his job as a DJ.

near the clubs where the most serious DJ-ing is done. On a visit to Spain last year, the first trip abroad for any of them, DJ Kingy – who followed his dad into this business two years ago after taking over the family record decks – worked just for fun almost every night. In the booth at the club, where he ⁶ .... (mix) records, he seems oblivious to the rest of the planet. The thing he ⁷ .... (find) the hardest, he admits, is making sure that the vocals from two records are not going at the same time. It is intense, tiring work, although he ⁸ .... (work) only one night a week for the last couple of weeks. But he seems completely absorbed by it, and has no intention of doing anything else.

Exam know-how

Paper 3 Part 3

- Follow the instructions carefully.
- Think carefully about the meaning of the first sentence. Identify any key structures.
- Don't change the key word.
- The key word may not be the part of speech you first think of.
- Count the words in your answer. Contractions like *don't* count as two words.
- Don't leave out any information in the first sentence.
- Look before and after the gap to check your answer fits grammatically.

1 Nicola was too tired to do her homework.
  that
  Nicola was .... not do her homework.
2 What attracts you to becoming a DJ?
  want
  Why .... a DJ?
3 Paul decided to join a band so left university.
  gave
  Paul .... to join a band.
4 I can assure you that our lead singer does not intend to leave the band.
  intention
  Our lead singer .... the band, I can assure you.
5 Sam wrote his first hit single for the band last year.
  was
  The band's .... last year by Sam.
6 I'm sure the musicians' performance was one to be proud of.
  must
  The musicians .... their performance.
7 Last year the band earned less than in previous years.
  as
  Last year the band didn't .... as it had in previous years.
8 Rod started work here a year ago.
  since
  Rod .... last year.
9 Kate began studying music two years ago.
  for
  Kate .... two years now.
10 The actors' rehearsal for tonight's play is still going on.
  finished
  The actors .... for tonight's play yet.

Listening skills

PART 2 NOTE-TAKING

1 Decide which answers a–j belong with which questions 1–10 in 2 below. Which is the most likely answer in each pair?

2 🎧 You will hear a dancer, Joanna Mendes, talking about her life **HELP** and work. For questions 1–10, complete the notes.

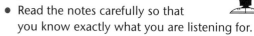

Exam know-how

Paper 4 Part 2
- Read the notes carefully so that you know exactly what you are listening for.
- You don't need to worry about notes fitting grammatically into a complete sentence.
- The answers may be just one word.
- Try to predict the answers but remember that they may not be what you expect.

Joanna Mendes – dancer

a Italy / the theatre

b fast food / chocolate

c reading / horse-riding

d doctor / actress

e 13.7.69 / 30.7.99

f get divorced / get married

g happy / tired

h modern dancing / disco dancing

i fascinating / boring

j local / National dance school

Favourite treat: 1 ....

Date of birth: 2 ....

Profession of mother: 3 ....

Attitude towards education: found school 4 ....

Prize she won: a place at the 5 ....

Worst critics: those in 6 ....

Best performances: 7 ....

Preferred means of relaxation: 8 ....

Attitude towards work: makes her 9 ....

Future plans: 10 ....

3 Were your predictions in 2 correct?

Spelling: the *schwa* sound

4 🎧 The word *perform* has two syllables (*per/form*) but the first syllable is not stressed, and the vowel is pronounced /ə/. Listen to some other words from the text containing the *schwa* sound and write them below.

a ....

b ....

c ....

d ....

e ....

f ....

g ....

What about you?

5 Answer these questions.

a What impression do you think Joanna gives of the life of a professional dancer?

b What do you think you will be doing this time next year?

Speaking skills

PART 2 THE LONG TURN
Comparing photographs

1 Read the task and underline the most important words, then close your book and try to remember the task.

> These photographs show people working in the media. I'd like you to compare and contrast these photographs, and say what you think it would be like to do these jobs.

2 Look at these two photos and add to the list of points below.

Points to mention

What is similar about the photographs, e.g. people involved in the news, reaching a large audience.

....
....
....
....

3 Look again at the task in 1 and the photos in 2. Which of questions a–c do you think the listening candidate might be asked after his/her partner's long turn? Remember that the response should be brief, no longer than 20 seconds.

   a What problems do you think people might have doing jobs like these?
   b Would you like to do a job like these?
   c Why do you think people enjoy working in the media?

4 With a partner, you are going to do the task in 1 but with the pairs of photos on page 116 and 117. First, make a list of points to mention for each pair. Ignore the questions below the photographs.

5 Using the linkers below and the lists you made
HELP in 4, take it in turns to talk about your pair of photographs. Your partner will stop you after a minute and briefly answer the question below your photographs.

Comparing photographs

Both pictures ... but the first one ... .

In this picture ... but in this one ... .

This one ... , on the other hand, the second one ... .

This looks easier/more difficult/enjoyable because ... .

Revise and extend

lay and *lie*

▶ Extension p44/45 Text

1 Complete the other parts of the verbs, then use the correct forms to complete sentences a–h.

Infinitive	Past simple	Present participle	Past participle
lay (put)	....	....	....
lie (be situated)	....	....	....
lie (not tell the truth)	....	....	....

a Paris .... on the river Seine.
b Ted .... in bed all day yesterday – he was too lazy to get up.
c Please don't .... to me! I want to know exactly what happened.
d I think Bill .... about his age when he went for his interview.
e Could you .... the book on the second shelf?
f I was .... on the sofa when the phone rang.
g The hens have .... six eggs today.
h I was .... the dining room table when I heard a strange noise in the kitchen.

Expressions with *home*

▶ Extension p44/45 Text

2 Match these expressions with meanings a–g, then use some of them to complete sentences 1–5.

'Home is where the heart is.'
home truths
a home from home
home and dry
make yourself at home
'There's no place like home.'
bring (something) home to someone

a a place where you feel as comfortable and happy as if you were at home
b safe and successful after some difficulties
c behave as if you were at home
d make someone realise something or see a situation more clearly
e Home is the best place of all.
f honest criticism which may hurt, but which is meant to help
g Home is the place you feel most emotionally attached to.

1 What Jim said really .... to me how hard I need to work.
2 I told my brother a few .... and he wasn't very happy!
3 Please .... Don't ask before you use anything.
4 Once I had reached the last mile of the race I was ....
5 I stayed with some friends in the city and it was a real .... They were so kind to me.

Words connected with buildings

▶ Revision p45 Ex4

3 Write words which mean the same as definitions a–g. The first letter and the number of letters is given.

a a place where monks live
m __ __ __ __ __ __ __ __
b a flight of stairs inside a house
s __ __ __ __ __ __ __
c the opposite of 'floor'
c __ __ __ __ __ __ __
d places to put books
s __ __ __ __ __ __
e what is needed to supply electricity
w __ __ __ __ __
f the part of the house on the same level as the road
g __ __ __ __ __ __ f __ __ __ __
g what you might find on the floor in the bathroom
t __ __ __ __

▶ Extension p45 Ex4

4 Explain what each of a–h is like.

a bungalow
b semi-detached house
c detached house
d terraced house
e skyscraper
f studio flat
g mansion
h cottage

Phrasal verbs with *put*

▶ Extension p45 Ex5

5 Match the meanings a–d with the phrasal verbs in 1–4.

a save
b connect by telephone
c return to its proper place
d delay

1 If you hang on a minute, I'll put you through to the Managing Director.
2 I'm going to try and put something by for a rainy day.
3 I'm afraid the conference has been put off until next month.
4 Could you please put all these socks away in the chest of drawers?

6 Use one of the phrasal verbs in 5 to answer questions a–d using complete sentences.

a How important do you think it is to save money?
b Do you return things to their proper place in your own room?
c What sometimes happens when you ask someone to connect you to another person on the telephone?
d What would you do if you heard that your examination date had been delayed?

Writing

▶ Revision p44/45

7 Write a short paragraph with the title *The most interesting building I have ever been in*. Explain why you found it so interesting.

Present perfect simple or continuous?

▶ Revision p48

8 Use these verbs in the present perfect (simple or continuous) to complete 1–10.

become	know	get	travel	complete
rehearse	lose	meet	be	perform

Luke ¹ .... all morning. He
² .... a member of our band for about five months now but I ³ ....
Luke as a friend for much longer than that. It's the second band Luke ⁴ .... (ever) .... with but he says the members are the nicest people he
⁵ .... so far in the music business.
For the last few days, we ⁶ ....
ready for a concert up north. We ⁷ ....
all over the country for months now and we're all getting tired of being on the road. What we're all looking forward to is having a holiday when we
⁸ .... our next tour. I sometimes feel that, because we ⁹ .... quite well known, we ¹⁰ .... our right to have private lives of our own.

Past simple or present perfect?

▶ Revision p48

9 Put the verbs in brackets in a–h into the correct tense: past simple or present perfect.

a I .... (live) here for six months.
b When .... (you/move) to Spain?
c How long .... (you/have) your new mobile phone?
d We .... (buy) a new car last week.
e This is the first time I .... (ever/see) this film.
f .... (you/visit) South America before?
g I .... (go) to a disco last Saturday.
h What .... (you/do) to your hair? It looks awful!

MODULE 3b

Reading skills

PART 3 MISSING SENTENCES

1 Answer these questions.

a Do you enjoy shopping? Why/Why not?

b Do you agree that we have become a consumer society?

2 Read the article, ignoring the gaps, and find out what the most important influence on consumers is.

3 Seven sentences have been removed from the article.

CHECK Choose from the sentences A–H the one which fits each gap (1–6). There is one extra sentence which you do not need to use.

A These will arrive in the shops soon after a new show is on the air.

B Some consultants believe that if you can attract a child to a soft drink or a particular shop, he or she will stick with it throughout their lives.

C Supermarkets have learned to place merchandise strategically so that it can just about be grabbed from the seat of a trolley.

D In the past few years, marketing to children has grown into a huge global industry.

E Clothes have become a very important part of the business as children no longer wear hand-me-downs and jumpers knitted by their grandmothers.

F In addition, families are smaller, which means more resources for each child.

G Well, breaking into it involves an understanding of what makes them tick, what amuses and entertains them and how peer pressure is created in the playground.

H Not bad going when you consider it is only a few years since that first hit single came out.

Words connected with buying and selling

4 Match a–f with their contrasting meanings 1–8. One word has three contrasting meanings.

a spend	c consumers	e sales
b demand	d income	f increase

1 manufacturers	4 suppliers	7 save
2 expenditure	5 decrease	8 purchases
3 supply	6 producers	

I'm Britney

■ **The last few years have seen an explosion in the pre-teen sector of the consumer marketplace. Matthew Lynn reports**

In one ranking of the most powerful celebrity brands, pop star Britney Spears ranked fourth, behind the *Beatles*, Tom Cruise and Tiger Woods. [0][H] In what seemed like no time at all, she developed into a
5 major worldwide recording artist and also branched out into film acting and novel writing. Crucially, Spears also became the uncrowned queen of the burgeoning pre-teen market. Her earnings have been estimated at around £27m.

10 [1][ ] The stakes are so high that companies now compete fiercely for every last penny of pocket money, relying on the 'pester-power' of their target audience to put pressure on parents to part with ever-larger sums.

15 There are several powerful forces fuelling the boom in the children's market. First there has been an increase in disposable income, which means more money is available. [2][ ] Lastly, parents are far more generous about spending money on their
20 offspring than their own parents were with them.

One other factor: there is a growing appreciation among companies of the power of 'cradle-to-grave marketing'. In effect, it's a catch-them-young strategy. [3][ ] A five-year-old persuaded by a
25 particular brand, for example, could be worth thousands of dollars in profits in years to come.

So how do companies get a slice of the kids' market? [4][ ] Just like the adult market, the kids' market has its own divisions, namely, babies (the under twos),
30 'pre-tweens' (two to seven) and 'tweens' (eight to twelve).

In every segment of the market, TV is the most important tool. Advertisements in breaks create

...buy me!

demand for the spin-off products from TV programmes. [5] After that, it is the children who drive the sales. The kids have seen it on TV, and they ask their parents for it. But it is the adult who makes the final purchasing decisions, so companies have to make sure that it appeals to them as well, that it has the right moral tone, and best of all that it is educational.

Marketing to children goes through a complex process. It may start with television, but it moves on swiftly to the shops, which is where the kids can actually start pestering their parents. [6] Likewise, garage shops put chewing gum where youngsters can reach it while their parents are paying for petrol.

The Spears phenomenon illustrates the way in which marketing to children has changed over the past few years. It now resembles the adult market far more closely, and reflects the fact that children have become far more media saturated. There are now numerous channels aimed at kids and 'tween' markets on digital television, and dozens of magazines in circulation. The children's market has come of age – the genie has risen out of the bottle and is unlikely ever to be put back.

35
40
45
50
55
60

Exam know-how

Paper 1 Part 3
Complete the advice.
- Always read .... first for gist.
- Read sentences A–H and find words which ....
- Even if you think you know the answer, always try .... in each gap to make sure it doesn't fit.
- Try the .... again to make sure you don't really need it.

5 Use words from 4 to complete sentences a–j. There may be more than one correct answer.
  a We are please to announce a huge .... in the amount of goods sold this year.
  b I've managed to .... enough money to go on holiday this year.
  c This CD player doesn't work. I am going to write to the .... and complain.
  d It is the right of .... to return faulty merchandise.
  e There is no longer any .... for this type of mobile phone.
  f The company was unable to .... us with the computers we wanted.
  g Our .... figures show that the business has done well this year.
  h Our annual .... is much greater than our earnings, so we are in trouble!
  i .... of fresh vegetables can have financial difficulties if the weather is bad.
  j We have no items in stock as we are waiting for a delivery from our ....

Phrasal verbs with *come*

6 What does *come out* (sentence H) mean? Choose the correct word to complete the verbs in a–d, then match them with their meanings 1–4.

  a We came *against/across* a fantastic clothes shop in a small town we were visiting yesterday.
  b I hate to tell you this but we have come *off/up against* a rather serious problem.
  c Sarah wanted to arrange a picnic for her birthday but it didn't come *down/off*.
  d The price of petrol never seems to come *down/off*.

  1 be faced with
  2 be reduced in cost
  3 find or meet by chance
  4 happen/be successful or effective

Text talk ...
- Do you agree that if you attract a child to a product or shop they will stick with it for life?
- Are there any kinds of advertising that should be banned?

Writing skills

PART 2 REPORT

1 Read the question below and complete the mind map with your ideas.

```
┌─────────────────────┐     ┌─────────────────────┐
│ .................... │     │ .................... │
│ .................... │     │ .................... │
│ .................... │     │ .................... │
│ .................... │     │ .................... │
└─────────────────────┘     └─────────────────────┘

        Your college is
       improving its premises
       and the directors have
      asked you to write a report
       suggesting what facilities
        might be popular with
         students. Write your
          report in 120–180
                words.

┌─────────────────────┐     ┌─────────────────────┐
│ .................... │     │ .................... │
│ .................... │     │ .................... │
│ .................... │     │ .................... │
│ .................... │     │ .................... │
└─────────────────────┘     └─────────────────────┘
```

2 Read the report ignoring the gaps and any mistakes. Were any of the ideas similar to yours? Write suitable topic headings for paragraphs 1–4. Write a suitable opening and closing sentence.

3 Find and correct seven mistakes in the report.

Making recommendations

4 You can make recommendations in a report using *should* and the passive infinitive. Rewrite sentences a–e as in the example, using the openers given.

Example:
Installing a lift would be a good idea.
A lift should be installed.

a It would be nice to decorate the classrooms in pale colours.
The classrooms ....

b You could use one room for a café.
One room ....

c You could offer private lessons in the evenings.
Private lessons ....

d You must consider every possibility.
Every possibility ....

e Make sure you advertise the school in the local paper.
The school ....

REPORT

1 ....

What students need are large classrooms with big windows. This helps them to be concentrate better. In addition, a lift should be installed to the classrooms on the top floors. This would be good idea.

2 ....

I suggest to have classes in the mornings, afternoons and evenings becuase students could then choose to study at different times.

3 ....

I would also recommending a library where students can study on their own. There could be tapes, CDs and books for the students to lend.

4 ....

Last but not least, I suggest that you having a coffee bar or small café where students could meet and talk to each other.

Emphasising a point

5 You can emphasise something by using *What* at the beginning of the sentence and the verb *to be*. Rewrite sentences a–d as in the example.

Example:
Students need large classrooms.
What students need are large classrooms.

a Students really like somewhere to meet.
....

b We mustn't forget that students enjoy working on their own.
....

c It is important that the school has the right atmosphere.
....

d We should remember that it is difficult to please everybody.
....

Writing a report

6 Read the question and complete a mind map with your ideas (the pictures below may help you). Write your report using words and expressions from 4 and 5 and the Writing checklist below.

CHECK

> A new leisure centre is being built in your area and you have been asked to write a report suggesting what facilities might be popular with local people. Write your report in 120–180 words.

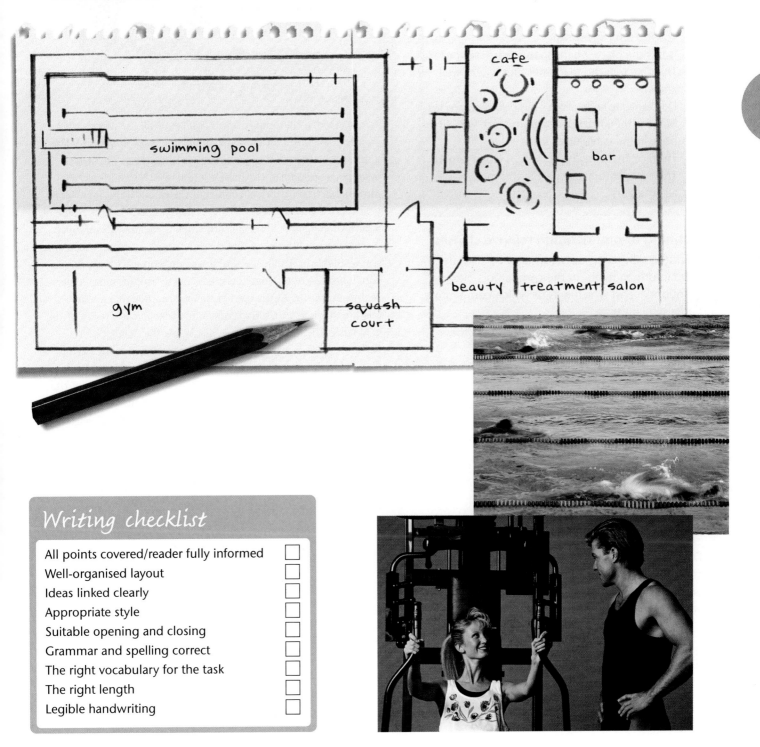

Writing checklist

All points covered/reader fully informed	☐
Well-organised layout	☐
Ideas linked clearly	☐
Appropriate style	☐
Suitable opening and closing	☐
Grammar and spelling correct	☐
The right vocabulary for the task	☐
The right length	☐
Legible handwriting	☐

Use of English skills

RELATIVE CLAUSES AND PRONOUNS

Defining or non-defining relative clauses?

1. Decide which sentence below, a or b, gives us extra information about the competitors already mentioned, and which tells us which competitors had a difficult time.

    a The competitors who took part in the cross-country ski race had a difficult time.
    b The competitors, who took part in the cross-country ski race, had a difficult time.

2. Decide which sentence, a or b, gives us extra information about the dogsled race already mentioned and which tells us which race has an interesting history.

    a The dogsled race which takes place in Alaska has an interesting history.
    b The dogsled race, which takes place in Alaska, has an interesting history.

3. Decide in which relative clauses in 1 and 2 you can use *that* instead of the relative pronoun. Can you leave out the relative pronoun in any of the sentences? Why?

4. Read the text opposite and complete 1–8 with these pronouns.

    > who   which   that   whose   where

    In which spaces is more than one answer possible? In which can you not use *that*?

The Iditarod race

The Iditarod, a National Historic Trail, runs all the way to Nome on a course [1] .... used to be an old dog team mail route. The annual dogsled race, [2] .... name is the same as the trail's, takes place in some of the remotest and most beautiful terrain imaginable. The historical context of the race is important. Many years ago, it was dogsleds [3] .... came to the rescue of Nome in a marathon against life and death when medicine was urgently needed for an outbreak of diphtheria. A small amount of medicine was available in Anchorage but it was not enough for the whole population. Most of Nome's citizens had to wait for more to be sent from Seattle. At the turn of the last century this was a bustling town [4] .... had come into existence as a result of the gold-rush. The area, [5] .... is just below the Arctic Circle, became cut off every autumn when ice formed over the Bering Sea. The only form of transport to the outside world was by dog team. The medicine was despatched first by rail to the end of the line [6] .... it was collected, then transported by relays of handlers and dog teams, [7] .... spared no expense in delivering their precious package. Faced with winter darkness and brutal temperatures [8] .... plunged to −50 degrees C, some 20 handlers and over 100 dogs made the courageous 1,100 km dash in five and a half days. The epidemic was broken and the dogs and handlers became the symbols of Alaska.

Using defining relative clauses

5. Match the sentence halves using a suitable relative pronoun.

    a Over to your right you can see the park ...
    b Peter Rowlands is the researcher ...
    c This is a statue of the man ...
    d The two villages on either side of the river are joined by a narrow stone bridge ...

    1 ... invented the light bulb.
    2 ... was built by the Romans.
    3 ... article appeared in yesterday's newspaper.
    4 ... the weekly market is held.

6 Combine the sentences in a–d using defining relative clauses and suitable relative pronouns.

a I met a man yesterday. He was an historian.
The man ....

b We went on a guided tour. It was fascinating.
The guided tour ....

c A woman showed us round. She knew a lot about history.
The woman ....

d We watched a film. It lasted about 20 minutes.
The film ....

Using non-defining relative clauses

7 Use the notes in a–e to make sentences containing non-defining relative clauses and a suitable relative pronoun.

Example:
Peter the Great (Tsar 1672–1725) – modernised Russia.
Tsar Peter the Great, who lived from 1672 to 1725, modernised Russia.

a Heroditus (Greek) – the first historian

b Printing machines (appeared in Europe about 1450) – people exchanging ideas more easily

c Titian (paintings world-famous) – lived in Italy/16th century

d Gustavus Adolphus (King of Sweden 1611–1632) – made Sweden powerful nation

e Shah Jahan (Emperor of India) – built Taj Mahal in 17th century

PART 3 KEY WORD TRANSFORMATIONS

8 For questions 1–10, complete the second sentence so that it has a similar meaning to the first sentence, using the word given. Do not change the word given. You must use between two and five words, including the word given.

> **❗ Look out for (2)**
> - nouns ↔ verbs
> - relative clauses
> - the passive
> - conditionals
> - **different phrases with the same meaning**
> - reported speech
> - conditionals

1 The helicopter rescued everyone on board the ship.
rescue
It was a helicopter that .... of everyone on board.

2 The annual race is held in March.
place
The race .... is held in March.

Complete the advice.
- Follow the .... carefully.
- Look for any .... in the first sentence.
- Read what comes before and after the gap to make sure ....
- Don't change the .... or leave out ....
- The key word might not be ....
- Count .... carefully. Remember that .... as two words.

3 The town is not a major port nowadays.
be
The town .... a major port.

4 Medicine was urgently needed for the sick.
need
They were .... for the sick.

5 No one could reach the area in winter.
off
The area .... civilisation in winter.

6 We had too little medicine to treat everyone.
not
There .... us to treat everyone.

7 There was no other transport besides horses and carts in the area.
form
Horses and carts were .... in the area.

8 It was necessary to send supplies from abroad.
be
Supplies .... from abroad.

9 What attracts you to this part of the world?
find
What .... this part of the world?

10 The spectators dashed enthusiastically towards the winner of the race.
dash
The spectators .... towards the winner of the race.

Listening skills

PART 2 NOTE-TAKING
Predicting what you will hear

1 🎧 You will hear an interview with Mary Pagnamenta, who went on an unusual horseback ride in New Zealand. For questions 1–10, complete the notes.

[CHECK]

Exam know-how

Paper 4 Part 2
Match the sentence halves.

- Notes are not complete sentences, so ...
- Sometimes the answer may be ...
- The answers may be different from ...

a ... just one word.
b ... what you expect.
c ... don't worry about the words fitting grammatically.

MARY'S NEW ZEALAND HORSEBACK RIDE

Aim of ride: raising money for disabled children and hospital for [1] ....

Time taken: [2] ....

Distance covered: [3] ....

Companions on the trip: 20 disabled children & two [4] ....

Problems at the beginning: rain & lack of [5] ....

Most foolish mistake: setting out without a [6] ....

Most frightening experience: [7] ....

Most enjoyable Christmas celebration: [8] ....

What she learned: [9] .... herself.

Hopes for the future: stay in New Zealand [10] ....

2 🎧 These answers to questions 1–10 were written after the first listening. They are all wrong. Listen to the recording again and say what they refer to.

1 horses ....
2 six months ....
3 a few kilometres ....
4 boys ....
5 clothes ....
6 friend ....
7 meeting a bull ....
8 walking in sunshine ....
9 avoid taking risks ....
10 for a year or so ....

What about you?

3 Answer these questions.

a Would you consider doing what Mary did? Why/Why not?

b What would you like to do if you could take some time off work or studying?

Speaking skills

PART 2 THE LONG TURN (A GROUP OF 3)
Words with similar meanings

1 Find words with similar meanings in the list below. Which words can be used to describe the photos in Task 1 below, and Task 2 on page 118?

plastic mac	instructor	mountains
orchestra	teacher	slopes
pupils	shower	raincoat
students	sunshade	garden umbrella
downpour	band	

Task 1

2 In a group of 3, make a list of words for the Task 3 pictures on page 115. Can you think of other words with similar meanings?

Exam know-how

Paper 5 Part 2
Circle the correct information, a or b.

- The pairs of photographs and the tasks will be
  a completely different from each other.
  b theme-related to each other.
- As you look at the photographs, quickly think of
  a one thing.   b a few things to say.
- If you finish too quickly,
  a say 'That's all'.   b think of something else to say.
- When the examiner reads out your task
  a listen carefully so you know what to do.
  b ask the examiner to repeat it.
- When you answer the question after your partner's long turn you should speak
  a for a minute.
  b briefly and for no more than 20 seconds.

3 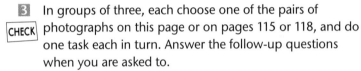 In groups of three, each choose one of the pairs of photographs on this page or on pages 115 or 118, and do one task each in turn. Answer the follow-up questions when you are asked to.

Task 1 *Student A*
Compare and contrast these photos, and say how the weather is affecting what the people are doing.

Question for Student B
What kind of weather do you prefer?

Task 2 *Student B*
Compare and contrast these photos, and say how useful you think it is to learn to do these things.

Question for Student C
Which of these things would you like to do well?

Task 3 *Student C*
Compare and contrast these photos, and say how you think the people in the queues are feeling.

Question for Student A
Do you think queues are a good idea?

4 Decide which of suggestions a–f would improve your performance, and why the others are not a good idea.
  a If you don't understand what you have to do, ask the examiner to repeat the task.
  b If you can't think of anything to say, keep saying the same thing repeatedly.
  c Look at your watch to see how much time is left.
  d Ask the examiner how much time you have left.
  e Relate the pictures to your own experience.
  f If you can't remember how to say something in English, ask the examiner what the word is.

Revise and extend

Verbs and prepositions

▶ Revision p54/55 Text

1 Use these prepositions to complete sentences a–f. Some may be used more than once.

> with   to   for   into   on

a I don't like spending money .... designer clothes.

b Who paid .... the tickets last night?

c Does this style of trainer appeal .... you?

d The company decided to branch out .... the teenage market.

e Children often put pressure .... their parents to buy things they see on TV.

f Selling to 'tweens' has grown .... a huge industry.

The verbs *rise, arise* and *raise*

▶ Extension p54/55 Text

2 Decide which verb means

- lift up or increase something.
- move upwards or become higher or stronger.
- begin to exist or appear.

Complete the table, then use the correct forms to complete sentences a–f.

Infinitive	Past simple	Past participle
rise	....	....
arise	....	....
raise	....	....

a The cost of living .... sharply since last year.

b Does the sun always .... at 6 o'clock in the morning?

c One or two problems .... yesterday because some of the goods delivered were faulty.

d At the meeting last week, we .... the question of an increase in salary.

e The cost of renting accommodation seems to be .... at an alarming rate.

f A thick column of black smoke began to .... from the burning building.

Words connected with buying and selling

▶ Extension p54 Ex4

3 Match these words with the meanings in a–h, then use them to complete sentences 1–8.

> priceless   worthless   a bargain   a rip-off
> earnings   goods   a rise   cash

a salary

b an increase (in pay)

c bank notes and coins

d something bought at less than its market price

e having no value or use

f something that costs much more than it ought to

g products

h of great value

1 I asked my boss for .... but she refused to give me one.

2 Look what I bought yesterday! Designer shoes for a few dollars – they were such ....

3 Be careful you don't drop that vase. It's absolutely ....

4 Surely you didn't pay so much money for a watch like that? What .... !

5 The dealer said these stamps were worth a lot of money but unfortunately they turned out to be ....

6 Sam's .... for the year weren't enough to finance a family holiday.

7 We only accept .... or cheques, not credit cards.

8 If any .... are found to be defective, a full refund will be given.

Phrasal verbs with *come*

▶ Revision p55 Ex6

4 Match the meanings in a–d with phrasal verbs 1–4.

a find or meet by chance

b be faced with

c take place or be effective

d be reduced in cost

1 come down

2 come across

3 come up against

4 come off

▶ Extension p55 Ex6

5 Match these meanings with the phrasal verbs in sentences a–d, then use the phrasal verbs to complete 1–4.

> happen   become ill with
> break into pieces   think of

a The children have come down with measles.
b How did the accident come about?
c James finally came up with an idea for saving money.
d This remote control has come apart. Do you think you could mend it?

1 Some children's toys .... much too easily.
2 Have you ever .... a great idea?
3 How do so many accidents in the home .... ?
4 The twins have never .... with any serious childhood illnesses.

Writing

▶ Extension p54/55

6 Write a short paragraph about an advertisement which you think is particularly effective. Say

- where you have seen the advertisement
- what it is for, why it appeals to you
- how successful you think it might be in selling the product.

Defining relative clauses

▶ Revision p58/59

7 Complete sentences a–h using one of the defining relative clauses 1–8 and a suitable relative pronoun. In which sentences can the relative pronoun be left out?

a The film .... last night was incredibly funny.
b The restaurant .... turned out to be cheaper than we had expected.
c The sightseeing tour .... was rather boring.
d The guide .... was a qualified historian.
e The man .... was not allowed on the plane.
f The street .... was very noisy.
g I haven't had time to read those books ....
h What was the name of the man .... ?

1 we went on
2 passport had expired
3 the hotel was situated
4 we saw
5 you lent me
6 showed us round
7 gave the talk at the conference
8 we had a meal in

Non-defining relative clauses

▶ Revision p58/59

8 Combine sentence halves a–g with 1–7 to make sentences with non-defining relative clauses and a suitable pronoun.

a This island was discovered only a few years ago.
b The President is visiting Russia tomorrow.
c Edinburgh castle is an important historical monument.
d Our organisation is helping to reduce pollution in city centres.
e Long ago, the King used to come here in the summer with his courtiers.
f The painter Van Gogh lived for many years in Paris.
g I got a good mark for my homework.

1 It was built hundreds of years ago.
2 He spent most of the year in a palace in the capital.
3 It is situated in the Pacific Ocean.
4 His work can be seen in a new exhibition.
5 His private plane left this morning.
6 It was set up about 20 years ago.
7 I did my homework on the bus.

Reading skills

PART 3 MISSING PARAGRAPHS

1 Read the article, ignoring the gaps, and find out where the Cayman Islands are and who Arthur is.

2 Seven paragraphs have been removed from the article. [HELP] Choose from the paragraphs A–H the one which fits each gap (1–6). There is one extra paragraph which you do not need to use.

A Eventually he swam away confidently and enthusiastically. Although the same could scarcely be said for all the other 303 turtles, some of whom seemed totally confused by the entire episode.

B If you want to lie on this beach, don't let the reputation for mixed weather put you off. The islands are safe in most storms.

C Nevertheless, if you treat them with respect and (better still) if you feed them, they are quite happy to be held by visitors in search of unusual photo-opportunities. The one I held felt rather like an oversized Portobello mushroom.

D Happily, in the end, all the turtles seemed to get the hang of it. We all stood watching as 303 heads bobbed up and down in the sunset, moving gradually out to sea.

E The event is financed by an organisation which was originally set up in the late 1960s. It is now the largest project of its kind in the world.

F A small child told me he had named his turtle Chocolate and, apparently in sympathy, my partner named hers Milky Bar. Given the tendency of chocolate to be eaten, those names seemed to be tempting fate.

G A minimum contribution of $15 – which can be paid over the internet before your visit – allows you to adopt one of these creatures. It also enables you to deposit it in the shallow waters off the Safehaven beach.

H Not that this is unusual in the Cayman Islands. Bear in mind that Seven Mile Beach is so called because it's five and half miles long. Against that background, it soon becomes pretty clear that it's best not to take things at their face value.

Escape from Paradise

We arrived at the Cayman Islands shortly after Hurricane Michelle had swept by. Waiting for us was our host, who was taking us on a catamaran ride to visit Suzie, Daisy and their friends. These improbably named females are stingrays that hang out about four miles from the coast of Grand Cayman in an area called Stingray City. It's a ridiculously inappropriate name because 'city' creates images of traffic jams and skyscrapers, whereas this is a quiet corner of the Caribbean Sea, very near the reef.

0 **H**

At Stingray Bar you can stand waist-deep in the warm water and play footsie with these gentle, peace-loving creatures which don't sting (that's another misnomer). However, their sharp tails will give you a nasty cut if you kick them. Quite right, too!

1

The stingrays did not seem to be any the worse for wear after Hurricane Michelle's passage. Nor did 303 aquatic creatures we had the privilege of meeting on the first Friday of November. This was the Islands' annual turtle freedom day, an occasion that nobody should miss.

2

In order to study their behaviour in their natural habitat, each year the organisation tags and releases from its farm about 1,000 one-year-old green turtles, some of which have been seen as far afield as Venezuela and the United States. Most of these are released privately, but each year residents and visitors can join the fun (and support the research initiative by sponsoring a turtle, i.e. paying to release it into the wild).

3

For the animals themselves, being picked is the equivalent of winning the lottery. Instead of living on the farm for the rest of their lives, they are instantly given licence to roam freely throughout the waters of the Caribbean. Unsurprisingly, the
30 turtle release is an especially popular event among children, for whom it is also an educational one. Many of the youngsters we met at Safehaven had formed emotional bonds with their chosen turtles.

4

I wanted something that sounded more solid, so mine ended
35 up with Arthur, although as I carried him towards the sea, I'm not sure who was in a more advanced state of panic. Arthur was palpitating furiously, while I was terrified of dropping the poor creature at a vital moment in his life.

5

One paddled in a small and comical semi-circle on the beach's
40 edge, soon returning to land after apparently having decided that he was not looking forward to the opportunity of exploring his new home.

6

As Arthur and his chums explored their new accommodation for the first time, we strolled back through the golf course at
45 Safehaven to ours.

Text talk...

♦ Would you like to visit a place like the Cayman Islands?

♦ How important is animal conservation?

Exam know-how

Paper 1 Part 3
- Read the main text first to see how it develops.
- Read the missing paragraphs and try to work out what the main idea in each one is.
- Read what comes before and after each gap in the text before deciding which paragraph fits best.

HELP

Using adverbs

3 Make adverbs from these adjectives, then use the adverbs to complete sentences a–h. Besides *-ly*, you may need to add other letters to the words.

enthusiastic	total	free	special
furious	scarce	gradual	original

a After their release, the turtles were able to swim .... and without fear.
b What you are saying is .... untrue!
c All the children shouted .... that they would love to learn how to scuba dive.
d Pat's dog swam .... against the strong current.
e This building was .... a boat house.
f These shoes were .... made for me in Italy.
g We have .... any money left for holidays this year.
h Some of the turtles .... made their way down to the sea but it was a long, slow process.

Verbs of movement

4 Match these verbs from the article with meanings a–e, then use them in the correct form to complete sentences 1–5.

sweep	roam	paddle	stroll	bob

a move up and down quickly
b move or push with force
c wander
d walk in a leisurely way
e move or walk in shallow water

1 In this part of the park, animals are allowed to .... around wherever they like.
2 We could just make out the seal's head .... above the waves.
3 After its owner had thrown a stick into the pond, the dog .... out to fetch it.
4 A huge wave .... everyone on deck off their feet.
5 Jim and Barbara .... to the water's edge and watched the sun setting over the sea.

Writing skills

PART 2 DISCURSIVE COMPOSITION

1 Read the question opposite and decide which of the plans (A or B) you think is better. Say why.

2 Decide why Victor's composition on page 67 would not get a good mark in the exam. Use the Writing checklist to help you.

3 Read these two paragraphs from Maria's composition and compare them with Victor's. Write two final paragraphs for Maria's composition using these paragraph openers.

- On the other hand, ...
- So, in conclusion, I would argue that ... .

Does watching television have some useful purpose, or is it just a waste of people's time?

If people choose carefully what they watch, they will find programmes that are not only entertaining but educational, too. after a hard day at school or at work, everybody needs to relax and watching television is an excellent way to do so. We can also learn a lot from watching programmes like the news, documentaries, wildlife series and programmes about history. Television can make these subjects come alive and make us more interested in learning about them.

Gerunds and prepositions

4 Complete sentences a–e using the verbs in brackets in the gerund form and one of these prepositions.

> of   with   for   in   on

a Most people are interested .... (watch) the news on TV.

b I am not keen .... (listen) to the radio.

c You cannot blame people .... (want) to relax in the evenings.

d Some people are fed up .... (see) the same programmes all the time.

e People can easily get tired .... (sit) in front of the TV.

Your class has recently had a discussion about television. For homework, your teacher has asked you to write a composition in 120–180 words giving your opinions about the following statement:

Watching television is a waste of people's time.

PLAN A

Paragraph 1

Introduction – how much time I spend watching TV

Paragraph 2

Programmes I like

Paragraph 3

Programmes my parents hate

Paragraph 4

Say that TV is a good thing

PLAN B

Paragraph 1

Introduction – how much time some people spend watching TV

Paragraph 2

The benefits of watching some programmes

Paragraph 3

The reasons why watching TV may be a waste of time

Paragraph 4

Say whether watching TV is a good or bad thing

Victor's composition

Watching television is very popular and a lot of people like to spend their time watching it.

I prefer go to the cinema. There are a lot of films that I enjoy and the special effects are excellent. Also I like to go out with my friends and not stay at home. We can enjoy ourselves and eat popcorn.

My parents are watching a lot of television but they are watching programmes I don't like. They are tired at the end of the day so it doesn't mind what they watch. For them it isn't really waste of time.

So I think that watching television is waste of time for me.

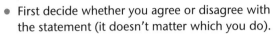

Exam know-how

Paper 2 Part 2
- First decide whether you agree or disagree with the statement (it doesn't matter which you do).
- Express only one side of the argument or express views for and against.
- Write a plan before you begin.
- Beginning with a question can make the introduction more interesting.

Expressions with *make*

5 What does the expression *make something come alive* in Maria's composition mean? Match these other expressions with *make* with definitions 1–5.

a It is easy to *make a habit of* staying in at night.

b People seem to have lost the art of *making conversation*.

c Sometimes I cannot *make up my mind* what to watch.

d We need to *make the most of* our leisure time.

e Many people *make do with* entertainment at home.

1 decide

2 get used to

3 gain as much advantage as possible

4 talking to each other

5 manage with something which is not satisfactory

Writing a composition

6 Using Plan B on page 66, do the following task. The Writing checklist will help you.

HELP

Your class has recently had a discussion about reading. For homework your teacher has asked you to write a composition in 120–180 words giving your opinion about the following statement:

Reading is an excellent way to improve your knowledge.

Writing checklist

All points covered/reader fully informed	☐
Well-organised layout	☐
Ideas linked clearly	☐
Appropriate style	☐
Suitable opening and closing	☐
Grammar and spelling correct	☐
The right vocabulary for the task	☐
The right length	☐
Legible handwriting	☐

Use of English skills

PART 4 ERROR CORRECTION

1 Read the text, ignoring any mistakes you come across, and find out how the emergency services managed to rescue the Pennsylvanian miners.

2 For questions 1–15, read the text and look carefully at each line. Some of the lines are correct, and some have a word which should not be there. If a line is correct, put a tick (✓) by the number. If a line has a word which should not be there, write the word at the end of that line.

HELP

Examples: 0   ✓   00   so

Emergency services win through

   0 Exhausted and soaked in coal-blackened water, but apparently

 00 so well enough to joke about their ordeal, nine miners were

   1 hauled to the surface in a small Pennsylvanian town. It was ....

   2 the end of a 77-hour operation by the emergency services to ....

   3 free them out from the flooded subterranean chamber where ....

   4 they had have been trapped. Above ground, a team of rescuers ....

   5 were drilled an oxygen hole to pump warm air to the men. Nothing ....

   6 had been heard from those trapped underground for the almost 24 hours, ...

   7 when the first drill hit hard rock and being broke, delaying the procedure ....

   8 for another 18 hours. The rescuers could do a little else except wait for ....

   9 a giant mechanical drill to be transported from West Virginia. The ....

 10 frustrated rescuers then they began to bore a second hole using the drill ....

 11 which had finally been delivered. Ground water levels were now falling ....

 12 25cm an hour, thanks to the use of compressed air. Eventually, after ....

 13 one by one, beginning just before 1 a.m. local time, the miners were ....

 14 brought to the surface in a yellow capsule which measuring 66cm across. ....

 15 Their first of words to the rescuers were: 'What took you guys so long?' ....

> **❗ Look out for (1)**
> - prepositions
> - articles
> - auxiliary verbs
> - relative pronouns

PAST PERFECT TENSE

Correct any incorrect statements about the past perfect.

a It is rarely used in English.
b It is used for an action which happened before another in the past.
c It does not have a continuous form.
d The negative form is *hadn't* or *had not* + past participle.

Ordering events

3 Beginning with the example, put events a–j from the text opposite in order.

a The miners found themselves trapped in the rising water. ☐
b Rescue workers began drilling an oxygen hole. ☐
c The drill from West Virginia arrived. ☐
d The miners were hauled to the surface. ☐
e Rescuers started drilling a second hole. ☐
f *The miners went to work underground.* 1
g The miners were finally able to joke about their experience. ☐
h The place where the miners were working started to flood. ☐
i The first drill broke. ☐
j Underground water levels started to fall. ☐

Past simple or past perfect?

4 Make one sentence from each pair in a–e using one verb in the past simple, one in the past perfect, and the words in brackets. Make any other necessary changes.

a (just after)
The shaft reached a depth of 30m.
The drill struck hard rock and broke.

b (because)
A telephone was lowered into the shaft.
The miners were able to talk to their rescuers.

c (after)
The courageous miners were eventually rescued.
The miners were trapped for three days.

d (who)
The families were grateful to the rescue services.
The rescue services brought the miners to safety.

e (once)
The rescue workers were encouraged.
The rescue workers heard the miners tap on the pipe.

Paper 3 Part 4

● Read the text once quickly, then again carefully sentence by sentence (not line by line).
● There are usually about five correct lines.
● Check the possible extra word does not refer to something else in the sentence.

Past perfect simple or continuous?

5 Say which verb in italics suggests that the action lasted for some time, then put the verbs in brackets in sentences a–e into the correct form of the past perfect.

The police *had been asking* local people questions to find out if anyone *had witnessed* the accident, when they received the anonymous phone call.

a Speaking a short time after the residents .... (rescue) by fire-fighters, local people were full of praise for the emergency services.
b A spokesperson at the local hospital, where some residents .... (take) for a check-up, said that everyone who .... (bring in) was doing well.
c Apparently, prior to the flooding, the miners .... (accidentally/break) through to an abandoned mine, which .... (mark) on the map as being 90 metres away.
d One miner who .... (work) near the surface managed to escape.
e The trapped men were described as heroes because they .... (warn) other miners of the flooding as soon as it happened.

Find the extra word

6 Find the unnecessary word in each of sentences a–e.

a Before being called to the fire in the warehouse, the fire crew had been rescued an old lady's cat.
b How long had you been waiting at the bus stop before the bus had arrived?
c The police praised for the members of the public who had helped them with their enquiries.
d The fire-fighters were in the great danger of being overcome by smoke.
e Temperatures were dropped to zero and heavy snow fell overnight.

Listening skills

PART 3 MULTIPLE MATCHING
Focusing on key words

1 Look at the task in 2 and underline the key words in each sentence A–F. Are the statements for or against building new airports?

2 🎧 You will hear five local residents talking about a plan to build a new airport near where they live. For questions 1–5, choose which of the opinions A–F each speaker expresses. Use the letters only once. There is one extra letter which you do not need to use.

HELP

A We should accept the problems new airports cause.

B Many people don't realise how noisy aeroplanes are.

C We shouldn't build airports near residential areas.

D We don't really need to build any more new airports.

E People don't want to make up their minds about new airports.

F We shouldn't be putting more flights in the air.

Speaker 1 ☐ 1

Speaker 2 ☐ 2

Speaker 3 ☐ 3

Speaker 4 ☐ 4

Speaker 5 ☐ 5

3 🎧 Listen to one sentence from each extract and complete a–e with words used to express opinions.

a .... airports as such, or even the noise planes make.
b But it's the safety aspect I ....
c There's .... that we have to find somewhere to build another airport.
d I'd .... to live near an airport if it wasn't for the almost continuous roar of aeroplane engines.
e I know most people .... that planes are noisy and they pollute the atmosphere, but you've got to move with the times, haven't you?

What about you?

4 Answer these questions.

a How would you feel if a new airport was going to be built where you live?
b Do you agree that flying is the transport of the future? Why/Why not?

Speaking skills

PARTS 3 AND 4 THE COLLABORATIVE TASK AND DISCUSSION

1 Put a tick next to each of activities a–j you would expect to do in Part 3.

a Turn-take

b Invite your partner to speak

c Start a conversation

d Express your own opinion

e Give personal information

f Reply to your partner's questions

g Ask the examiner questions

h Agree or disagree

i Make a suggestion

j Reach a decision

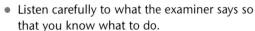

Paper 5 Part 3

- Listen carefully to what the examiner says so that you know what to do.
- Each Part 3 task has two parts: the first is talking about the visuals, and the second is usually making a decision. Don't forget about the second part.
- Ask for your partner's opinion.
- Talk about all the pictures or images before making your final decision.
- Speak clearly so that the examiners can hear you.

2 Look at pictures 1–7 opposite, then read the task on page 118. Write down the following information.

a Length of task: ....

b What the pictures show: ....

c What to talk about: ....

d What to decide: ....

3 With a partner, do the task in 2. Time yourselves for three minutes and see if you can talk about each picture and come to a decision in the time allowed. Use some of the phrases below, or others of your own.

HELP

Starting a conversation

So, shall we begin with this one?

Let's start then, shall we?

Right. I think we could start with this picture.

Inviting your partner to speak

What do you think?

What's your opinion?

What about you?

4 🎧 What happens in Part 4 of the test? Listen to the recording, which is also on page 115, and decide whether the candidates' answers are suitable or not.

5 Answer these questions.

a Do you think it is possible to be happy all the time?

b Which is better: being part of a large or small family?

c How important is it to have a lot of interests and hobbies?

d How long do you think school holidays should be?

Revise and extend

Using adverbs

▶ Revision p65 Ex3

1 Write the correct form of words a–f in a suitable place in each sentence.

a total   I disagree with what you say.

b original   This road was built by the Romans.

c gradual   The procession made its way through the town.

d free   Deer wander in this area of the park.

e special   This book was written for students taking examinations.

f enthusiastic The crowds cheered as the film stars began to arrive.

Verbs of movement

▶ Revision p65 Ex4

2 Write verbs of movement which mean the same as definitions a–e. The first letter and the number of letters is given.

a wander   r _ _ _ _ _

b walk in a leisurely way   s _ _ _ _ _ _

c move or walk in shallow water p _ _ _ _ _

d move or push with force   s _ _ _ _

e move up and down quickly b _ _

3 Use one of the words in 2 in the correct form to complete a–e. Some words are in the noun form.

a Can you see that object .... up and down in the sea. What is it?

b Do you fancy a .... through the park?

c The enormous bird .... down from the top of the hill to the valley below.

d Small children love to go for a .... in the sea.

e Wild animals should be allowed to .... in their natural surroundings.

Expressions with *get*

▶ Extension p64/65 Text

4 Unscramble the letters in italics to find the verbs with *get*, then match them with the possible meanings.

a It can sometimes be difficult to get your message *rossac* to a large audience.

b I don't understand how the thieves managed to get *yaaw twih* the robbery.

c Rainy days really get me *nowd*.

d How John managed to get *roughth* his driving test I shall never understand.

e Why don't we get *thegerot* for a meal sometime?

> meet   pass   make people understand
> make someone feel unhappy
> do something bad and not be caught

5 What does *get the hang of it* mean? Choose the correct meaning of the verbs in a–e and answer questions 1–5.

a Maria gets on well with the other students in her class.
  • is making progress • has a friendly relationship with

b Sally never seems to get round to doing her homework until it's too late!
  • find the time to do • visit her friends and do

c I tried to get out of helping Dad to wash the car but it didn't work.
  • go outside • avoid

d Our dog died last year and my little sister just can't get over it.
  • recover from • get away from

e Paul was getting nowhere with his revision.
  • had nothing to do • was not making progress

1 How well do you get on with your neighbours?

2 What would you like to get out of doing? (Why?)

3 What often helps people to get over an illness?

4 What can you do if you think you are getting nowhere with your studies?

5 What kinds of things do you never get round to doing until it's too late? (Why?)

6 Use one of the verbs in 5 to complete sentences a–e.

a To be honest, nothing really .... me .... I think I must be an optimist!

b It's almost impossible for anyone to .... theft when security is as tight as this.

c Although the exam seemed difficult, most people appear to have .... it.

d Frances and I always .... for a drink after work when we lived in Paris.

e The government seems to be .... its message .... at last.

Different kinds of creatures

▶ Extension p64/65 Text

7 Explain what a–e mean, then match them with creatures 1–6.

a mammal   c reptile   e herbivore
b carnivore   d insect

Comparisons with animals

▶ Extension p64/65 Text

8 Complete expressions a–f with the names of animals, then match the expressions with meanings 1–6.

a Mark's got a memory like a(n) .... He never forgets anything.

b It must be pouring outside. You look like a drowned ....

c My sister hates her new school. She says she feels like a(n) .... out of water.

d Sometimes the twins fight like .... and .... but they are very fond of each other.

e Paula has taken to basketball like a(n) .... to water.

f I don't like our new boss. She watches everyone like a(n) ....

1 be in the wrong environment
2 disagree or argue violently
3 not forget things that happened a long time ago
4 look very carefully and critically at what people do
5 get used to something quickly and easily
6 be very wet

Writing

▶ Extension p64/65

9 Imagine that you have a family pet and are going away on holiday for two weeks. A friend has very kindly offered to look after your pet while you are away. Write a list of instructions. Mention

- food
- sleeping habits
- what to do if the pet is ill
- any exercise you normally give your pet

Past simple or past perfect?

▶ Revision p69 Ex4

10 Put one verb in the past simple and the other in the past perfect in sentences a–h.

a My grandfather often .... (wish) he .... (go) to university.

b I .... (know) that I .... (make) a mistake in my maths test.

c I .... (buy) the shoes that I .... (see) in the shop window the day before.

d Although I .... (never drive) a car before, I .... (seem) to know exactly how to do it.

e For one awful moment we .... (think) we .... (forget) our passports.

f Yesterday Martin .... (tell) me that Susan .... (pass) her exams.

g We .... (visit) Spain many times before we .... (decide) to buy a flat there.

h After I .... (finish) school, I .... (go) on a trip around Europe.

11 Put the verbs in 1–10 into the correct form.

Last night the emergency services [1] .... (call) to a fire which [2] .... (start) in a hotel in the town centre 20 minutes earlier. When they [3] .... (arrive), they [4] .... (find) that most of the guests [5] .... (already/evacuate) from the hotel. Unfortunately, one elderly guest, who [6] .... (not hear) hotel staff banging on his door just after the outbreak of the fire, [7] .... (be) still in the building. Luckily, however, fire-fighters [8] .... (manage) to rescue him just in time. Apparently he [9] .... (be) a fire-fighter himself before retiring last year, so he [10] .... (know) that he was in safe hands.

Reading skills

PART 4 MISSING PARAGRAPHS

1 Answer these questions.

a What are the main differences between watching a film at the cinema, on TV, or on video/DVD? Which do you prefer?

b What makes a film an Oscar-winner?

2 CHECK Seven paragraphs have been removed from the article. Choose from the paragraphs A–H the one which fits each gap (1–6). There is one extra paragraph which you do not need to use.

A Once you had a fix on the story, however, it was simply a question of sitting back and keeping tabs on the chief characters, united in their bravery, who are split into three groups. These groups didn't actually meet again in this second part of the trilogy and this was sometimes confusing, but it added variety to the scenes.

B These violent sequences were breathtaking. The conflicts were conducted with great ferocity and seemed much better than those I'd seen in other great movie epics over the years.

C As my daughter later pointed out, the role of the females in the film was simply to flee with the children and the old folk. When the beautiful aristocratic Eowyn decided she wanted to take up arms, she was informed by her uncle that the fighting should be left to the men.

D We needn't have worried. We were forced to sit through about twenty minutes of adverts and trailers before the long-awaited feature film began. By this stage, the children were getting restless, and the supplies of popcorn were rapidly dwindling. But our patience was rewarded, and the cinema audience was reduced to a hushed silence.

E The film concluded with a cliffhanger that aimed to have us all sitting in the same seats to see how it all turned out in the concluding part, *The Return of the King*.

F I had read the author's books when I was much younger and for me they had a magical quality. I was curious to see how successfully they would capture the sinister but spell-binding story of the hobbits and their fight against the forces of evil.

THE LORD OF THE RINGS

Film critic Roger Jackson takes his family to see the second film in the epic trilogy.

I first went to the cinema when I was about four years old. I still remember it vividly. I'm one of five children and we were on holiday by the seaside. It was windy and wet – a typical summer-holiday afternoon. We all piled in there armed with
5 bags of sweets, glad to be indoors, and excited at the thought of the cartoon film that we were about to see.

0 **H**

I'll never forget that initial thrill of my first visit. I was reminded of it when I decided to take my own three children to see one of the winter's new releases, *The Lord of the Rings:*
10 *The Two Towers*, starring Sir Ian McKellen. My wife had taken them to see the first of the fantasy trilogy based on the stories of J.R.R. Tolkien, so it was now my turn.

1 ▮

The visit started off badly. The film was released in the winter and when we arrived at the cinema in the freezing cold, we
15 found a queue stretching round the car park. We were actually quite surprised when we eventually made it to the ticket office, and even more so when we managed to buy four seats together. We hastily bought popcorn and practically ran to find our seats before the film began.

2 ▮

20 I slowly began to realise that anyone in the audience unfamiliar with the first part of the trilogy, *The Fellowship of the Ring*, would have a hard time trying to work out who the

G Howard Shore's background music is truly amazing. He has used both emotion and imagination to produce a musical score which reflects the story brilliantly.

H At home we had a small TV, so what we saw on the big screen was truly amazing. It was the first time we had all sat for more than half an hour in silence – a real treat for my mother and father.

characters were, what the plot was about, and how the film held together. It was expected that we would know the story
25 about a dangerous mission to destroy an evil magical ring.

3 [ ]
There was no girl playing a leading role in any of these bands of steadfast characters, and this second film found far more work for its screen heroes than its heroines. Certainly, there was nothing like the elf maiden Arwen's marvellous
30 horseback rescue of Frodo Baggins, which had been a major highlight of the earlier picture.

4 [ ]
Apart from the extraordinary plot and characters, we were treated to a stunning visual epic with plenty of battles. In fact, there were enough battles packed into three hours to
35 keep the audience on the edge of its seat almost continuously. The warriors, mostly digitally created, seemed to go into battle every couple of minutes.

5 [ ]
As well as the action-packed script, there was also some good acting. The speech made at the end by brave, honest
40 hobbit Sam, about the struggle of good against evil, was moving. But I thought the ending itself was one of the most memorable moments.

6 [ ]
There was no doubt in the minds of my children that they would be there once again, waiting with bated breath. It
45 occurred to me later that none of the three had stirred or moved from their seats in the whole three hours. If proof was needed of the quality of the film, this was it! Nothing else could have held the children's attention for so long!

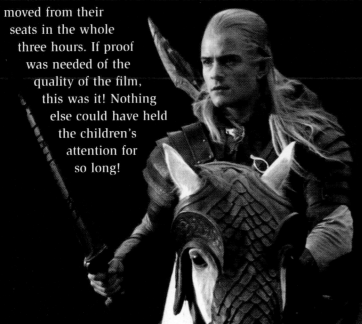

Paper 1 Part 3
Answer the questions.
- How will reading the main text first help you?
- What should you try to work out for each missing paragraph?
- What should you check before making your final decision?

Words connected with the cinema

3 Use words a–g to complete sentences 1–7.
a new releases e trailer
b screen f starring
c background music g leading role
d acting

1 If you watch the .... , you have some idea as to whether you want to see a film or not.
2 I prefer to watch films on a big ....
3 The .... can help to create atmosphere in a film.
4 Sometimes the .... of the main characters is not as good as the special effects.
5 A star in a .... can make millions of dollars.
6 I remember seeing an enjoyable romantic comedy .... Hugh Grant.
7 I never get round to seeing .... – I wait until the films come out on video.

The verb *hold*

4 What does *held together* (line 24) mean? Match the phrasal verbs with *hold* in a–f with meanings 1–6.
a The bad weather held up my flight last night.
b A gang of masked robbers held up the bank in the High Street yesterday afternoon.
c John's illness held him back at school.
d The police tried to hold back the demonstrators.
e Do you want to hold on to the passports or shall I?
f Emily held on tightly to her father's hand.

1 grip 4 prevent from making progress
2 keep 5 cause delay
3 rob 6 prevent from physically moving forward

Text talk...

- Which films that you have seen have the best
  a background music?
  b special effects?

- Why do you think some good films are not box-office successes?

Module 4B 75

Writing skills

PART 2 DISCURSIVE COMPOSITION

1 Read this question and make a plan for the answer.

> As part of a project on life in the countryside and life in a city, you have been asked to write a composition of 120–180 words giving your opinions about the following question.
> *Why would anyone choose to live in a big city?*

PLAN

Paragraph 1
Introduction saying ....
....
....

Paragraph 2
Mention points for ....
....
....

Paragraph 3
Mention points against ....
....
....

Paragraph 4
Summarise whether ....
....
....

Nowadays, more and more people are deserting big cities and choosing to live in smaller towns. 1 .... is life in big cities really as bad as some people make it out to be?

It is a fact that living in a city has its disadvantages. 2 .... , the large amount of traffic means that there is a lot of pollution. 3 .... that because there are so many people, it is easy to feel isolated and not feel a part of the community. 4 .... , some cities are thought to be more dangerous than smaller places because a lot of crime takes place there.

2 Read the composition opposite, ignoring the spaces, and compare it to your plan in 1. How many points does the writer make for and against life in a city?

3 Complete gaps 1–10 in the composition using a–j. More than one answer may be correct.

a to sum up
b on the other hand
c so
d first of all
e secondly

f last but not least
g to begin with
h although
i finally
j another point is

Words with similar meanings

4 Find words in the composition which mean the same as a–j.

a greater numbers of
b leaving
c awful
d claim it is
e it is true

f lonely
g occurs or happens
h close
i dependable
j disadvantages

5 .... , there are many advantages to living in a large city. 6 .... , everything you could possibly want is nearby. 7 .... , public transport is usually cheap and reliable. 8 .... , there are far more job opportunities.

9 .... , we can see that 10 .... there may be many drawbacks to city life, there are also many advantages.

Making comparisons

5 There are three examples of comparisons in the composition: *as ... as*, *more ... than*, and *far more*. Using the information in a–e, make similar comparisons. You may need to change the order of the words.

a cities/villages
b people in small towns/big cities
c life in the countryside/city
d cost of accommodation in cities/towns and villages
e entertainment in cities/villages

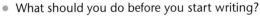 CHECK

Exam know-how

Paper 2 Part 2

Answer these questions.

- What should you do before you start writing?
- What can make your introduction more interesting?
- Does it matter if you agree or disagree with the point of view stated?
- Is it all right to express only one side of the argument?

Expressions with *feel*

6 *Feel isolated* and *feel a part of* appear in the composition. Match the expressions with *feel* in a–e with definitions 1–5.

a *Feel free* to say exactly what you think.
b Do you *feel like* going to the cinema?
c I don't *feel up to* going to school today.
d Getting a good mark in my composition made me *feel good*.
e Does it *feel strange* being back here after such a long time away?

1 want to
2 seem unusual
3 be happy
4 be ready to face or deal with
5 don't hesitate

Writing a composition

7 As part of the same project in 1, you have been asked

CHECK

to write a composition of 120–180 words giving your opinions about this question:

Why would anyone choose to do an outdoor job?

Write your composition using some of the ideas in this section. The Writing checklist will help you.

Writing checklist

All points covered/reader fully informed	☐
Well-organised layout	☐
Ideas linked clearly	☐
Appropriate style	☐
Suitable opening and closing	☐
Grammar and spelling correct	☐
The right vocabulary for the task	☐
The right length	☐
Legible handwriting	☐

Use of English skills

PART 4 ERROR CORRECTION

1 Read the text, ignoring any mistakes you come across, and find out what some people rely on to predict the weather.

2 For questions 1–15, read the text in 1 again and look carefully at each line.

CHECK Some of the lines are correct, and some have a word which should not be there. If a line is correct, put a tick (✓) by the number. If a line has a word which should not be there, write the word at the end of that line.

Examples: 0   would   00   ✓

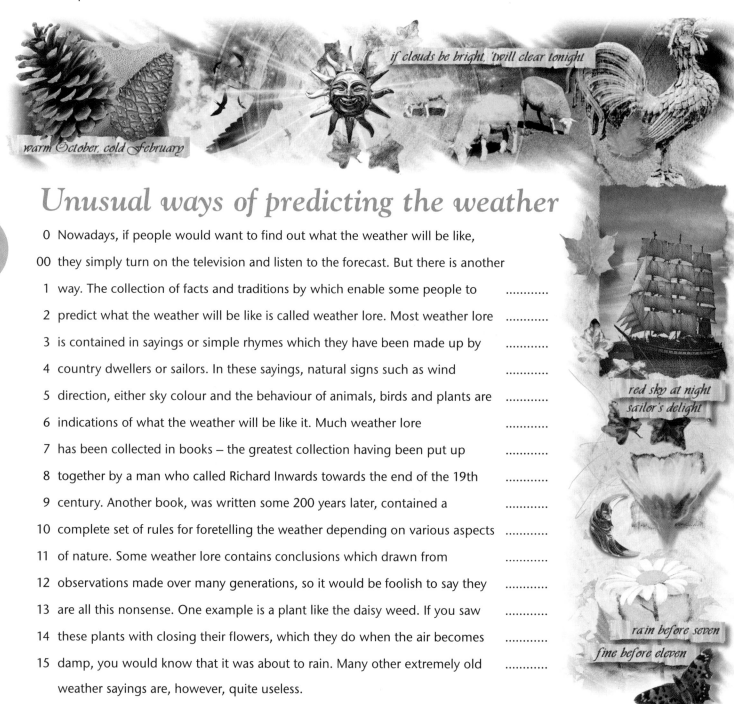

if clouds be bright, 'twill clear tonight

warm October, cold February

red sky at night
sailor's delight

rain before seven
fine before eleven

Unusual ways of predicting the weather

  0 Nowadays, if people would want to find out what the weather will be like,

00 they simply turn on the television and listen to the forecast. But there is another

  1 way. The collection of facts and traditions by which enable some people to   ....

  2 predict what the weather will be like is called weather lore. Most weather lore   ....

  3 is contained in sayings or simple rhymes which they have been made up by   ....

  4 country dwellers or sailors. In these sayings, natural signs such as wind   ....

  5 direction, either sky colour and the behaviour of animals, birds and plants are   ....

  6 indications of what the weather will be like it. Much weather lore   ....

  7 has been collected in books – the greatest collection having been put up   ....

  8 together by a man who called Richard Inwards towards the end of the 19th   ....

  9 century. Another book, was written some 200 years later, contained a   ....

10 complete set of rules for foretelling the weather depending on various aspects   ....

11 of nature. Some weather lore contains conclusions which drawn from   ....

12 observations made over many generations, so it would be foolish to say they   ....

13 are all this nonsense. One example is a plant like the daisy weed. If you saw   ....

14 these plants with closing their flowers, which they do when the air becomes   ....

15 damp, you would know that it was about to rain. Many other extremely old   ....

     weather sayings are, however, quite useless.

CONDITIONALS

Test your knowledge

Match questions a–e with answers 1–5.

a	How many different types of conditionals are there?	1	after *if*
b	Which conditional is used to talk about things which might happen in the future?	2	four
c	Which conditional is used to speculate about what happened in the past?	3	the third
d	In which part of conditional sentences do we not generally use *will* or *would*?	4	*had* and *would*
e	What two meanings does *'d* have in this conditional sentence? *'If you'd told me your secret, I'd have kept it to myself.'*	5	the first

Which conditional?

3 Match conditional sentences a–d with the explanations in 1–4.

a If you boil water, it turns to steam.
b If it's fine, we'll have a barbecue.
c If Ted were a millionaire, he'd give all his money away to the poor.
d If Daisy had worked harder, she would have got top marks in the test.

1 This is very unlikely to happen.
2 This is always true.
3 This definitely didn't happen.
4 This may happen.

The zero and the first conditional

4 Use the correct form of the verbs in brackets to complete these sentences. More than one answer may be possible.

a If you .... (drink) too quickly, you may .... (get) hiccups.
b If you .... (see) Debbie, ... (you/tell) her that I'll phone her this evening?
c You .... (get) soaked if you .... (go) out in this rain!
d The food .... (not/go) bad if you .... (keep) it cool.
e If you .... (finish) your homework, we .... (go) out.
f We .... (stop) and ask someone the way if you .... (forget) where the house is!

The second conditional

5 Say which of the second conditional examples in 1–3 is used to

a give someone advice.
b talk about something which can never happen.
c talk about something which is unlikely to happen.

1 If I were President, I could live a life of luxury.
2 If I were you, I would give up the idea of being an entertainer.
3 If I were an animal, I'd like to be a dolphin.

Exam know-how

Paper 3 Part 4
Answer these questions.

● After reading the text once, should you read it again line by line, or sentence by sentence?
● About how many lines are usually correct?
● What should you check about the extra word?

6 Complete second conditional sentences a–d using the correct form of the verb in brackets and ideas of your own.

a If I .... (have) the money, I .... (buy) ....
b I .... (live) if I .... (be) famous ....
c What .... (you/do) if you .... (win) .... ?
d If I .... (be) a lot younger, I .... (make) a few changes to my life, for example ....

The third conditional

7 Answer the questions about sentences a and b.

a If Patsy hadn't got up late, she wouldn't have missed the plane.
(Did Patsy get up late?)
b If Patsy had heard her alarm, she would have arrived in time to catch the plane.
(Did she arrive in time to catch the plane?)

8 Match the sentence halves in a–e and 1–5 to make third conditional sentences.

a Paul (not win) the lottery
b I (realise) the ice was so thin
c We (not break) down
d We (sit) somewhere else
e I (never move) into this flat

1 (have) the car serviced
2 (know) how noisy the neighbours were
3 (not go) skating
4 (be told) the seats were behind a pillar
5 (not go) to live in the Caribbean

Listening skills

PART 3 MULTIPLE MATCHING
Different words, the same meaning

1 The words you hear in the recording are often different from those you read in the options. Can you think of any words the speakers might use which mean the same as those in 1–5?

1 a argument
   b have a good relationship with
2 a annoy
   b friendly conversation
3 a intelligent
   b man
4 a sad or unhappy
   b 'gap' between younger and older people
5 a people who are very enthusiastic about something
   b say what will happen in the future

2 🎧 Listen to some sentences from the recording and check your answers in 1. Each speaker uses two words, a and b.

3 🎧 You will now hear the five people you heard in 2 talking about

CHECK close relationships they have with friends and family members. For questions 1–5, choose which of the opinions A–F each speaker expresses. Use the letters only once. There is one extra letter which you do not need to use.

A We waste a lot of time arguing.   Speaker 1 ☐ 1

B I only ask him for help if I have a serious   Speaker 2 ☐ 2
   problem.

C We have a lot of shared interests.   Speaker 3 ☐ 3

D He can be rather unreliable at times.   Speaker 4 ☐ 4

E I've learned a lot from him.

F I always tell him everything.   Speaker 5 ☐ 5

Exam know-how

Paper 4 Part 3
Complete the advice.
- As you listen to each extract, read ....
- Check that the extra option does not ....
- Changing your answer may ....
- Do not write more than ....
- Listen for the same information expressed ....

What about you?

4 Answer these questions.
a What kind of relationship do you have with your best friend?
b Which do you think is better – having a lot of friends, or a few close ones?

Speaking skills

PARTS 3 AND 4 THE COLLABORATIVE TASK AND DISCUSSION

1 Look at the pictures. What is the connection between them? What do you think the examiner might ask you to do in the Part 3 task?

2 🎧 Listen to the task without writing anything down, then see if you can remember what you have to do. You can also read the task on page 118.

Exam know-how

Paper 5 Part 3
Answer these questions.

- Why should you listen carefully to the examiner?
- Usually, how many parts are there to each task?
- When talking to your partner, what should you not forget to do?
- What should you do before making your final decision?
- Why is it important to speak clearly?

3 Match a–h with photos 1–7.

a water pollution	e species dying out
b noise pollution	f global warming
c traffic congestion	g getting rid of rubbish
d cutting down trees	h air pollution

4 In pairs, do the task in 2. Use the words in 3 and some of the phrases below.
CHECK

Expressing your own opinion

In my opinion, …

Personally, I think …

Actually, I don't think that …

Making a suggestion

Why don't we …?

What about choosing …?

I think we should talk about …, don't you?

5 Decide what kinds of questions the examiner might ask in Part 4. Now look at page 117 and answer the questions. Are they different from the ones you thought of?

Revise and extend

Words connected with the cinema

> Revision p75 Ex4

1 Write words which mean the same as a–f. The first letter and the number of letters is given.

a taking part in a film   a _ _ _ _ _
b films which have recently appeared   n _ _   r _ _ _ _ _ _ _
c where a film is projected   a s _ _ _ _ _
d what a star of a film has   the l _ _ _ _ _ _   r _ _ _
e short extracts advertising a film   t _ _ _ _ _ _ _
f something that creates atmosphere in a film   b _ _ _ _ _ _ _ _ _   m _ _ _ _

The verb *hold*

> Revision p75 Ex5

2 Use one of these verbs with *hold* in the correct form to complete sentences a–e.

> up   back   onto

a Have you heard that the bank in the High Street was .... yesterday?
b The police were unable to .... the crowds demonstrating against the government.
c Peter's injury .... him .... , and he wasn't chosen for the football team.
d Please .... my hand as we cross the road.
e The plane was .... by the air traffic controllers' strike.

Talking about films

> Extension p74/75 Text

3 Write sentences describing the features of a–f.

a a thriller
b a cartoon
c a black comedy
d a sci-fi film
e a super-hero film
f a musical

Adjectives ending in *-ed* and *-ing*

> Extension p74/75 Text

4 Say what the difference in meaning is between *interested* and *interesting* in these sentences.

a Sophie is interested.
b Sophie is interesting.

5 Use an appropriate adjective ending in *-ed* or *-ing*, formed from these verbs, to complete sentences a–h.

> amuse   fascinate   bore   terrify
> amaze   embarrass   distress

a I'm always .... when I watch horror films.
b When I saw *The Lord of the Rings*, I was .... by the special effects.
c Films about war are always ....
d I always feel .... if I start to cry at the cinema.
e Some romantic comedies are rather .... , but others are just downright ....
f It's .... how many extras were in this film!
g The audience wasn't .... by the black comedy.
h I wonder why some people find disaster movies so .... ? I can't stand them!

Phrasal verbs with *fall*

> Extension p74/75 Text

6 Match the phrasal verbs in a–f with meanings 1–6.

a If we spend all our money, we'll have nothing to fall back on in an emergency.
b The class had made plans to go swimming yesterday but they all fell through.
c By the end of the meeting they had all fallen in with the Chairman's suggestion.
d Our neighbours haven't spoken to us since we fell out two years ago.
e Pat and Martin fell for each other when they first met six months ago.
f We must buy some new furniture – these old chairs are falling apart!

1 agree to
2 have a disagreement
3 be attracted to
4 break into pieces
5 not succeed
6 rely on for support

7 Use the phrasal verbs from 6 in the correct form to complete sentences a–f.

a Despite some disagreement, everyone eventually .... our idea of going to the cinema.
b The seats in this cinema must be old. They are all .... !
c I'm afraid to say that Sue and I .... about what we are going to do tomorrow.
d What will we .... if we lose our jobs?
e Our plans to go to America last year ....
f Do you think you can .... someone the moment you meet them?

Writing

▶ Extension p74/75

8 Write a paragraph (about 150 words) about a good film you remember well. Say

- when you first saw it
- who you saw it with
- why you liked it
- how it is different from other films you have seen.

Making comparisons

▶ Revision page 77 Ex6

9 Complete sentences a–e with the correct missing word and an adjective of your own.

a The city is not .... as the countryside.

b The countryside is far .... the city.

c The cost of accommodation is .... in a small town .... it is in a large city.

d There is .... in a city than in a village.

e I don't like living in the .... as I like living in the ....

Expressions with *feel*

▶ Revision p77 Ex7

10 Write in the missing words in sentences a–e. The first letter of each word is given.

a Do you feel l............. going for a walk this morning?

b The swim in the sea made me feel g............. .

c Bob doesn't feel u............. t............. going out.

d Please feel f............. to tell me what you really think.

e Did it feel s............. visiting your childhood home?

Using conditionals

▶ Revision p79

11 Put the verbs in brackets in sentences a–g into the most likely form of the conditional: zero, first, second or third.

a If Rosy .... (not go) to university, she .... (not marry) her History lecturer.

b If I .... (be) a Hollywood film star, I .... (be) rich and famous.

c Metal .... (expand) if you .... (heat) it.

d We .... (go) for a picnic tomorrow if the weather .... (be) fine.

e If we .... (remember) to set the burglar alarm last night, we .... (not be robbed).

f If I .... (can) speak English perfectly, I .... (get) a job as an interpreter.

g If you .... (mix) the colours red and blue, you .... (get) purple.

12 Complete these sentences in your own words.

a If I were running the country, I ....

b If I have time, I ....

c If I hadn't been so lazy, I ....

d If I add too much salt to these potatoes, ...

e Would you marry me if.. ?

f What would have happened if .... ?

Find the extra word

▶ Extension p79

13 Find the unnecessary word in each of sentences a–h.

a If you will arrive early tomorrow, can you open all the windows in the classroom?

b If I were not you, I'd discuss the problem with my parents.

c Would you be mind if I asked you a question?

d If I had have known the answer to the question, I would have told you.

e We can go out if you have had finished talking.

f If you drop eggs, the shells are break.

g If you had been driving just a little more slowly, you could not have stopped at the traffic lights.

h Pete would have to been ready earlier if he hadn't spent so much time having a bath.

Reading skills

PART 4 MULTIPLE MATCHING

1 Answer these questions.

a How important are places like museums and art galleries?

b How much does it cost to go to museums and art galleries in your country? Should entry to them be free? Why/Why not?

2 Read the text quickly and find which country the writer thinks is best for viewing works of art.

3 Read the article again. For questions 1–13, choose from the places (A–G).

HELP

A Vienna
B Los Angeles
C Frankfurt
D Essex
E London
F Chicago
G Las Vegas

CUT-PRICE CULTURE

In which of the places A–G above are the following true?

0	Reductions are available for those still in education.	*E*
1	Your presence may be welcomed by professionals.	....
2	Entrance to some museums is now free.	....
3	No one expects you to pay for anything.	....
4	You could be invited to something you later regret going to.	....
5	If you are here on a certain day you can enjoy a museum without paying.	....
6	This cultural experience is what the artist expected it to be.	....
7	People don't expect this place to be full of culture.	....
8	Free culture is not necessarily desirable.	....
9	You need to be prepared to spend a lot here.	....
10	You could be caught unawares after visiting the works of art.	....
11	Your appearance could lead you to an unexpected opportunity.	....
12	Famous places seem to come together.	....
13	Culture is being used to reduce damage to property.	....

Text talk...

◆ Which of the cultural activities in the text would you be interested in?

◆ Some people say works of art should be returned to their country of origin. What's your opinion?

When the average traveller hears the word 'culture', they reach for their wallet. If you find yourself in Vienna with the chance to hear Mozart exactly as the composer intended, expect your credit card account to reach its own little crescendo when the statement
5　comes in. Quite right, too. A world that wants to enjoy creative genius must pay enough to sustain the artist in his or her next production. Art in all its glories does not come cheap. Or does it?

The cultured budget traveller is adept at finding freely available culture – which is more widely available than you think. Spend a
10　few days in Los Angeles, look like a clean-living sort of person with time on their hands, and you will soon be approached by someone offering free tickets. Often, these will be for a recording of some dreadful daytime TV show. But scouts often comb cinema queues for foreign backpackers, offering tickets to movie previews
15　at Hollywood's shimmering Directors' Guild. The previews are staged for critics, who apparently feel more comfortable being in the company of a randomly selected audience than in an almost-empty preview cinema. Backpackers find themselves in the unusual position of being extras in a movie audience rather than the film itself.

20　The crafty traveller also knows that there is an art (in every sense) to being in the right place at the right time. Should you find yourself with a spare day in Frankfurt, just hope that it is a Wednesday – when most of the world-class museums in Europe's financial capital welcome visitors for free.

25　The free provision of an art form is not always a blessing. In an attempt to curb vandalism at railway stations in the British county of Essex, the authorities have begun to broadcast light classical music free of charge on the station platform. This is not welcomed by all travellers.

30　Everyone knows that London isn't the cheapest place in the world to live. But most museums have recently dropped or brought down any charges they made. The bad news is that you may have to pay a little extra to see the best exhibitions, although you can get reduced rates with a student card.

35　Whatever you feel about removing art from its original surroundings, it's always a delight to see so many works of art in the same place at any one given time, and, in my experience, the USA does it best. The Chicago Institute of Art is one of the finest collections in the world – but if you step outside you'll be even
40　more surprised to find a more modern kind of sculpture, a superb Alexander Calder mobile.

But Las Vegas is the city that turns on its head the notion that you should have to pay for artistic entertainment. From the continuous acrobatics at Circus Circus, via the absurd pirate show at Treasure
45　Island to the sight of Paris, Venice and Luxor within a few blocks, Las Vegas is an unlikely culture capital of the world – if not for the more intellectual traveller, then at least for the budget traveller.

Exam know-how

Paper 1 Part 4

- Write the letters representing, e.g. the places, next to the text where they are mentioned to help you.
- Pencilling the question number beside the answer in the text will help you check your answers.
- Skim read the whole text quickly each time you answer a question.

Words which go together

4　Word combinations a–f appear in the text. Use them to complete sentences 1–6.

a credit card　　　d creative genius
b freely available　e financial capital
c classical music　f reduced rates

1　A truly successful artist needs to have
　.. .

2　Is it true that the ....
　of Europe is Frankfurt?

3　I find .... boring.
　I prefer jazz.

4　There are .... for
　students wishing to visit the museum.

5　Culture is .... in
　some cities, if you know where to look.

6　I don't own a ....
　because I think they encourage people to
　spend too much.

Phrasal verbs with *bring*

5　What does *brought down* (line 31) mean? Circle the correct second part of the phrasal verbs in a–d and match them with meanings 1–4.

a I'll bring your dictionary *back/off/down* to school tomorrow.

b Sam never thought he would win the race but he managed to bring it *back/up/off*.

c Someone brought *down/up/off* the subject of a rise in salary at yesterday's meeting.

d What brought *up/about/in* that outburst of anger?

1　cause to happen

2　return something to someone

3　make a success of something against all expectations

4　raise (in conversation)

Writing skills

PART 2 A SHORT STORY

1 Read the question and story opposite and complete gaps 1–8 with a–h. The words may be used in more than one answer.

a then
b as soon as
c for another fifteen minutes
d suddenly
e early in the morning
f when
g a few minutes later
h the moment

2 Number events a–j in the order in which they took place in the story. The pictures will help you. The first is done for you.

a We were told to change trains in Paris. ☐
b We saw that our train had vanished. ☐
c We went to buy some lunch. ☐
d *We booked our tickets from London to Marseilles.* ☐ 1
e We crossed Paris by taxi. ☐
f We realised that we hadn't missed the train. ☐
g We were told that the train had been moved. ☐
h We returned to the platform. ☐
i We asked a porter for help. ☐
j We boarded the train in London. ☐

Using a variety of tenses

3 Combine the pairs of sentences in a–f using the verbs in brackets in the past simple, past perfect, or past continuous tenses, and using sequencing words like *after*, *while* and *when*.

a We (travel) to Athens. The train (break) down.
....

b We (buy) our tickets. We (board) the train.
....

c The guard (ask) us for our tickets. We (have) lunch.
....

d We (arrive) in Milan. It (rain) heavily.
....

e We (spend) a few days in Madrid. We (travel) south.
....

f We (drive) to Portugal. We (have) a slight accident.
....

You have been asked to write a short story of 120–180 words for a school journal. The story must begin with these words:

You'll never guess what happened to me last month ...

You'll never guess what happened to me last month. Some friends and I were travelling from London to Marseilles by train. We left London ¹ ....

² .... we booked the tickets, we'd been told that we would have to change trains in Paris.

³ .... we arrived in Paris, we took a taxi to the south of the city, ⁴ .... boarded our train to the

Writing checklist

All points covered/reader fully informed ☐
Well-organised layout ☐
Ideas linked clearly ☐
Appropriate style ☐
Suitable opening and closing ☐
Grammar and spelling correct ☐
The right vocabulary for the task ☐
The right length ☐
Legible handwriting ☐

south of France. We 5 .... realised that we had not had lunch, so we decided to go and buy something for the journey.

6 .... we returned to the platform 7 .... , we couldn't believe our eyes. The train had disappeared. It had not been due to leave 8 .... Fortunately, there was a porter nearby and we asked him in our rather bad French what we could do.

To our surprise, he just smiled and told us not to worry. Apparently they had simply moved the train to another platform! Sure enough, there it was on platform 6, waiting to take us to Marseilles.

before/after/when/while + -ing

4 Instead of using tenses, you can use *after, when, while,* etc. + *-ing.* Use one of them and one of the verbs a–e in the *-ing* form to complete sentences 1–5.

a arrive   b cross   c book   d travel   e have

1 .... lunch, we went for a walk.
2 .... your tickets, ask for a reserved seat.
3 .... to Italy, we met some interesting people.
4 .... at the airport, we realised we'd forgotten our passports.
5 .... the road, remember to look both ways.

Exam know-how

Paper 2 Part 2
- Choose this question only if you enjoy writing stories and have had practice.
- List the events in the order in which they take place before you start writing.
- Use complex sentences to combine some of the events.
- Use topic vocabulary.
- Use an exclamation mark (!) to highlight the interesting part of the story.
- Don't make your story too complicated.
- Don't go off the subject.

The verb *change*

5 Use one of these words to complete the expressions with *change* in a–e, then match the expressions with meanings 1–5.

mind	money	subject
clothes	buses	

a We were told we'd have to change .... in London.
b You can't change your .... about going on holiday now. I've already booked the hotel.
c Please don't change the .... We need to discuss this now.
d Could you change this .... into Euros, please?
e I'd like to change my .... before going out to dinner.

1 put on something different
2 alter your decision
3 move from one to another
4 start talking about something different
5 exchange for the same amount

Writing a story

6 Write a story answering the question in 1.
HELP The Writing checklist will help you.

Use of English skills

PART 5 WORD FORMATION

1 Read the main text quickly and find out what the writer feels about how he spent his summer holidays when he was younger.

2 For questions 1–10, use the word given in capitals at the end of each line
HELP to form a word that fits in the space in the same line.

Summer holidays – past and present

My ⁰ ....._daily_..... summer holiday schedule consists of waking at 1 pm,   DAY

eating, showering, ¹ .... amusing myself for a few hours, then going   HAPPY

back to sleep at around 2 am. I sometimes wish it could go on for ever.

When I was about eight, living in New York, the long, steamy, hot summers

were the best time of the year. All the kids went on a day camp, ² ....   SENSE

dressed in T-shirts and swimming shorts. All the ³ .... was supervised   ENTERTAIN

by teenage Camp Counsellors. They took us on ⁴ .... trips to the pool,   END

cinema, and to basketball and baseball matches. Back in England, when I was

about 10, my parents ⁵ .... signed me up for football school, as well as   ENTHUSIASM

one week on a camp, which was ⁶ .... We did quad-biking and abseiling,   RESIDENT

amongst other ⁷ .... Looking back, I don't regret spending those weeks   ACTIVE

in sports complexes. They were definitely ⁸ .... , and they led to a   WORTH

great ⁹ .... in my sports and social skills. Things change when you   IMPROVE

become a teenager. Your parents tactfully suggest that you go to art

galleries and see ghastly plays you are studying at school, all of which

you consider to be completely ¹⁰ .... Once you get there, it's never   NECESSITY

that bad – but you'd rather be doing your own thing!

How many different forms?

3 Fill in the missing parts of speech of these other words from the text. There may be more than one answer and some words may not exist in every form.

Verb	Noun	Adjective	Adverb
a	....	amusing	....
b	....	different	....
c supervise	....	....	....
d sign	....	....	....
e regret	....	....	....
f consider	....	....	....
g	....	....	tactfully
h suggest	....	....	....
i think	....	....	....
j	....	....	completely

WISHES AND REGRETS

Correct the sentences which are incorrect.

a I wish I would be able to speak English perfectly.
b I wish my brother would stop playing loud music late at night.
c Paul wishes he were good at sports.
d We wish we have never gone on that holiday.
e We regret informing you that you have not been successful in your application.

regret (doing)/regret (to do)

4 Explain the difference between *I regret saying* and *I regret to say*, then make sentences using *regret (doing)* or *regret (to do)* for a–e.

a We're sorry to say that you have not been selected for the job.
b Diane isn't sorry she took up nursing.
c Bill and Tracy are sorry that they didn't move out of the city sooner.
d My aunt isn't sorry that she gave up smoking.
e The management are sorry to inform employees that redundancies are expected.

Expressing wishes about the present and the future

5 Find a sentence with *wish* in the text in 1, then use a–d to complete sentences 1–4.

a wasn't   b would   c didn't   d could
1 I wish Harry .... stop smoking but he won't.
2 I wish Harry .... stop smoking but he.
3 I wish Harry .... smoke but he does.
4 I wish Harry .... smoking a cigar but he is.

6 Add short sentences to a–j using *wish* and a verb in the past simple or continuous form, or *would*, beginning with the word given. More than one answer may be possible. The first one has been done as an example.

a I can't speak Japanese.
   I *wish I could* ....
b The teacher says the students talk too much during lessons.
   She ....
c George can't afford to buy a new car.
   He ....
d People are always sending me junk e-mails.
   I ....
e Paul never hands in his homework in time.
   The teacher ....

Paper 3 Part 5
- Read the text quickly for overall meaning.
- Read it again sentence by sentence to identify the parts of speech needed.
- Brainstorming all the parts of speech of the word in capitals may help you decide which word you need.
- You may need to add another word, e.g. *rain + drop = raindrop*.
- Check the context to see if the word should have a negative meaning, or needs a prefix or suffix.
- You will lose a mark if your spelling is incorrect.

f Tracy isn't studying history.
   She ....
g The children aren't enjoying this sightseeing tour.
   They ....
h Michael always leaves his dirty clothes on the floor.
   Michael's mother ....
i Susan never remembers to give Jack his messages.
   Jack ....
j Our bus never comes on time.
   We ....

Expressing wishes about the past

7 Say which of sentences 1 and 2 means

a I didn't do this but I now regret it.
b I did this but I now regret it.

1 I wish I had never bought the dress.
2 I wish I had bought the dress.

8 Decide which of these sentences is stronger in meaning.

a I wish I had remembered to lock the front door.
b If only I had remembered to lock the front door.

9 Express the ideas in a–j using the words in brackets.

a Tim and I didn't see the start of the film. (wish)
b My parents went to that new restaurant and it was terrible. (if only)
c My grandparents have never been abroad. (wish)
d My uncle and aunt say they were too young when they got married. (wish)
e Coming to live in this small town was not a good idea. (if only)
f Sam doesn't like that shade of blue he chose to paint his bedroom walls. (wish)
g I'm freezing in these summer clothes. (if only)
h The car we bought is just a heap of rust. (if only)
i My brother didn't get that job he applied for. (wish)
j I can't afford to rent a flat in town. (if only)

Listening skills

PART 4 THREE POSSIBLE ANSWERS
Listening for ideas expressed in different ways

1 🎧 Listen to some sentences from the recording in 2. How do the speakers express the following ideas?

a until you are exhausted ....

b I don't like it very much ....

c a lot of money ....

d really popular ....

e not so good for ....

f rather strange ....

g lots of things ....

h like the idea of ....

2 🎧 You will hear two friends talking about shops. For questions 1–7,
HELP decide which shop each statement refers to.

Write   **A**   for Addison's

       B   for Betterwear

or   **C**   for Clinton's

1 There is nowhere to park the car. ....

2 The clothes there are worth buying. ....

3 Goods there are cheap. ....

4 The international week was enjoyed by everybody. ....

5 You can't get many bargain breaks there. ....

6 The coffee is extremely good there. ....

7 There's a wide selection of sports goods. ....

What about you?

3 Answer these questions.

a Which is your favourite department store? Why?

b What future do you think there is for small, specialist shops?

Exam know-how

HELP

Paper 4 Part 4

- Listen for similar meanings but different words.

- When there are three possible answers, it doesn't matter who expresses the views. The important thing is what is said.

- The information on the recording is in the same order as in the questions.

❗ Never put more than one letter in each box. You will lose a mark even if one is correct.

Speaking skills

PARTS 3 AND 4 THE COLLABORATIVE TASK AND DISCUSSION

1 Where do you think the people in these three sets of photos are working? What jobs are they doing?

Exam know-how

HELP

Paper 5 Part 4

- Don't just give short answers – develop the topic.
- Don't talk across your partner – the examiners will not hear either of you.
- If the examiner asks your partner a question directly, don't answer it yourself.
- You may need to use a variety of tenses and structures to answer the questions in Part 4.

2 Discuss which of these you might need to do the jobs in 1–9.
a patience
b a sense of humour
c a friendly nature
d previous experience
e a head for figures
f communication skills
g special training
h physical strength

3 Read the task on page 116 and underline the most important words. Close your book and try to remember what you have to do.

4 In pairs, do the task in 3 using the words
HELP in 2 and some of the phrases below.

Reaching a decision
So let's make a decision, shall we?
So which ones are we going to/shall we choose?
Well, we both seem to agree that ...

Agreeing to disagree
Well, I don't really agree with ...
So we can't agree about ...
So we have different opinions about ...

5 In pairs, discuss these questions.
a What sort of jobs do you think are difficult to do?
b Which is more important, doing a job you enjoy or earning a lot of money?
c At what age do you think young people should leave school and start work?
d Do you think working people should have longer or shorter holidays than they do?
e Some people say our education does not prepare us for work. Do you agree?

Revise and extend

Words which go together
▶ Revision p85 Ex4

1 Use a–f to complete sentences 1–6.

a credit   d creative
b freely   e financial
c classical   f reduced

1 Culture is .... available in many towns and cities.
2 Where is the .... capital of the business world?
3 Do you think .... cards are a good idea?
4 Very few people have .... genius.
5 Can you tell me if .... rates are available for students?
6 I prefer rock and roll to .... music!

Phrasal verbs with *bring*
▶ Revision p85 Ex5

2 Match phrasal verbs a–d with meanings 1–4.

a bring up
b bring back
c bring off
d bring about

1 return something to someone
2 cause to happen
3 raise (in conversation)
4 succeed against all expectations

▶ Extension p85 Ex5

3 Replace the words in italics in a–e with phrasal verbs made from *bring* in the correct form and these words, then use the phrasal verbs to complete sentences 1–5 below.

| in | round | down | out | forward |

a The failure of their economic policy *defeated* the government.
b The council has *introduced* a tax on rubbish collections.
c Perhaps opening a window will *help* her *regain consciousness*.
d I'm afraid we have had to *move* the meeting *to an earlier time*.
e This fashion house is *producing* a new style of clothing.

1 The nurse tried unsuccessfully to .... the patient ....
2 I have .... your dental appointment .... so it's now on Monday instead of Tuesday.

3 Have you heard that they are .... a new law on smoking?
4 This new model sports car was .... only a few weeks ago.
5 Bad publicity was responsible for .... the new minister.

Reflexive pronouns
▶ Extension p84/85 Text

4 Reflexive pronouns are used when the object of the verb refers back to the subject, e.g. *teach yourself*. Use one of verbs a–f and a reflexive pronoun in the correct form to complete sentences 1–6.

a find   d enjoy
b teach   e blame
c help   f introduce

1 I don't think I could .... another language.
2 The students .... to the new teacher.
3 Don't all stand there waiting to be served. .... !
4 Sally often .... thinking of the house she used to live in.
5 We are going to .... , whatever the weather!
6 Ted .... for what happened.

Emphasising pronouns
▶ Extension p84/85 Text

5 Emphasising pronouns are used to stress that someone did something on their own, or without help. Use a suitable pronoun to complete sentences a–d as in the example.

Example: Dan decorated his bedroom *himself*.

a I wrote this poem ....
b If we can't find anyone to decorate the room we can always do it .... !
c The dog can switch the television on ....
d Did you know that DIY means do-it-....................... ?

Writing

▶ Extension p84/85

6　Write a short paragraph about a museum, art gallery or concert you have been to. Say

- where and when you went
- what you saw or heard
- how you felt about the experience
- whether you would go again.

I wish

▶ Revision p89

7　Make wishes about the past, present and future using the information in a–f, beginning *I wish ...* .

a　I forgot to do my homework last night.

b　I can't afford a holiday this year.

c　I haven't got time to go to the cinema tonight.

d　I didn't go to Sue's party. Apparently everyone had a great time!

e　I'm not very good at sport.

f　My parents are always telling me to work harder.

I wish and *If only*

▶ Extension p89

8　Put the verb in brackets into the correct form in sentences a–i. More than one answer may be possible.

a　I wish you .... (stop) interrupting me!

b　I wish I .... (have) three million dollars!

c　I wish I .... (can) speak English perfectly.

d　If only I .... (not have to) go to school!

e　If only I .... (do) my homework last night instead of going to the cinema!

f　I wish you .... (tell) me about the test yesterday!

g　I wish you .... (come) to the party tomorrow!

h　Jill wishes she .... (study) more last term.

i　I wish you .... (not give) me such expensive presents! You can't afford them!

Gerunds, infinitives and meaning

▶ Extension p89

9　Match the verbs in a–d with meanings 1–4.

a　I remember having picnics when I was a child.

b　I always remember to lock the door when I go out.

c　I tried turning the key in the lock gently but it still wouldn't open.

d　I tried to understand what the teacher was talking about but I couldn't.

1　I remember something, then do it.

2　I did something which I now remember.

3　I did it but it wasn't successful.

4　It wasn't possible for me to do this.

10　Use one of these verbs and the verb in brackets in the correct form to complete sentences a–g.

regret	remember	try

a　...................... (spell) everything correctly when writing a composition.

b　We .... (inform) you that your entry in the competition has not been successful.

c　Can you .... (go) on holiday as a child?

d　Please .... (post) my letter when you go out.

e　I .... (turn) the switch to the left but the heating still didn't come on.

f　I really .... (tell) my best friend what I thought of her new haircut.

g　I .... (not/put) more garlic in this pasta sauce.

Reading skills

PART 4 MULTIPLE MATCHING

1 What kind of career do you think would bring the greatest satisfaction? Why?

2 Quickly read the article to find out what job each person originally did and what jobs they do now.

3 Read the article again. For questions 1–10, choose from the people (A–D), and for questions 11–14, choose from the forms of alternative therapy (A–D).

CHECK

Which of the people suggest the following?

A Ian Miller   C Ann Wilkinson

B Chris Colgan   D Richard Kravetz

0 I feel equally stress-free as a pupil or as an instructor. ...*D*...

1 My work put a tremendous amount of pressure on me. ......

2 I had to work long hours.   ......

3 I hesitated about which alternative healing to take up. ......

4 I can use the skills I acquired in my previous job.   ......

5 I don't see any necessity for life's luxuries any more. ......

6 I find it frightening managing on a lower salary.   ......

7 I felt I wasn't contributing to society.   ......

8 I've encouraged others to find what suits them in life. ......

9 I was prepared to give up anything to achieve my goal. ......

10 I have a gift for sensing that something is wrong.   ......

According to the people in the article, which form of alternative therapy ...

A McTimoney chiropractic therapy

B Reiki life energy forces

C The Alexander Technique

D Yoga

can help you sleep?   ......

helped with a problem which wouldn't go away?   ......

has no ill-effects?   ......

was recommended by a colleague?   ......

WHAT MAKES someone with a high-flying career want to practise alternative therapy?

FRANCES IVE speaks to four former executives who did just that.

ALL CHANGE!

A Ian Miller

I realised that being an architect was not fulfilling enough for me. I wanted to give something back to the world and help people. As I learned more about life, I began to be attracted to the healing arts. 5 I had looked at a number of alternative therapies, but none of them felt right for me. One day, I visited the McTimoney chiropractic stand at an exhibition. This is a particularly gentle kind of therapy for the 10 manipulation of bones, which doesn't hurt, and their training offered the opportunity to work with animals. I took the three-year, part-time course, which involved one weekend a month and a lot of home study. 15 I was able to stay in my permanent job and maintain my income throughout the period, but once I had qualified, I worked part-time as both an architect and a chiropractor. After a few years, I gave up 20 the surveying and I'm now a full-time chiropractor. I earn nowhere near as much as I used to, but I wouldn't go back.

B Chris Colgan

25 I was director of Human Resources at a large internet service provider. It was hectic and demanding but I enjoyed the challenge. But I wasn't really fulfilled. I tended to focus on people I was working with, helping them to develop. I am an intuitive person and I can pick up when things aren't right for people. A woman who worked there suggested I became a reiki healer (that's

30 someone who uses life energy to heal the body with massage). She felt I might have the ability to do it well. So I started learning from a reiki master. People with aches and pains began appearing at my office doorway to ask me to give them some healing. One year, I went to the Arizona desert, and there I decided I couldn't

35 carry on doing my job. So I left a six-figure salary for an uncertain income. I don't regret it. I've met fantastic people and helped them change their lives and careers. Obviously, it's scary not earning so much money. But I'd rather be doing what I'm doing now.

C Ann Wilkinson

I didn't find working as a lawyer very rewarding. Apart from not
40 getting much satisfaction from it, it was incredibly stressful. A few years earlier I had had a recurring back problem and tried Alexander technique lessons. They train people to move properly and improve physical co-ordination without strain. I was very impressed. At this stage I didn't think it would be financially
45 possible to re-qualify as a teacher. But I became more interested in the technique and decided that it was worth any sacrifice and financial outlay. I gave up working for two years of the three-year course, and for the last year I worked part-time as a lawyer locally. The compensation was that the course was so great that
50 the rest ceased to be important. When you're doing something you're not really cut out for, you tend to need treats, things like expensive holidays. But when you do something you love, there's no need to escape from what you're doing. The training has completely changed me. My quality of life has improved hugely.
55 You can't put a price on that.

D Richard Kravetz

When I was training to be a chartered accountant, I used to take my work home and find my mind was so cluttered I couldn't switch off. I started going to yoga classes and found it stopped me waking in the night. After several years of attending classes, my
60 teacher, who was leaving, asked me to take over. Subsequently, I took a diploma in yoga, which was a two-year course. As time went on, my classes got bigger and now I run up to seven a week, which I fit round my accountancy. It brings balance into my life. Accountancy is a sedentary job, it's
65 money-driven and demanding. Yoga keeps me young and helps me relax. Even though I'm running the class, I am just as relaxed as if I were attending. My business experience made me confident
70 about running a class, and I love teaching.

Text talk...

◆ Why do you think some people decide they need a change in their lifestyle?

◆ What difficulties do you think you might face if you decided to retrain for a different job?

Paper 1 Part 4
Complete the missing information.
● When answering a question, you should skim read ....
● If you pencil in .... beside the information in the text, you can check your answers when you have finished.
● Some extracts may contain more than ....
❗ Finish the first task before doing the second or you may get confused.

Talking about work

4 Match comments a–f from the text with meanings 1–6.
a I wasn't really fulfilled.
b I was able to maintain my income.
c I was able to stay in my permanent job.
d I earn nowhere near as much.
e It was incredibly stressful.
f It was demanding.

1 I didn't have to leave full-time employment.
2 It required a lot of skill and effort.
3 I make much less.
4 I earned the same as I had before.
5 It put an amazing amount of pressure on me.
6 It didn't make me feel happy or satisfied.

Phrasal verbs with *cut*

5 What does *(be) cut out for* (line 51) mean? Use the context to work out the meanings of the phrasal verbs with *cut* in a–d, then use them to complete sentences 1–4.
a We will have to cut back on our spending if we want to go on holiday this year.
b I phoned Bill last night but we were cut off in the middle of our conversation.
c You'll have to cut out sugar from your diet if you want to lose weight.
d Please don't cut in when I'm speaking!

1 One member of the audience kept on .... while the speakers were talking.
2 Is there anything we could .... to try and save a little money?
3 I tried to shorten my composition by .... one of the paragraphs but then it didn't make sense.
4 There's something wrong with the lights. I think the electricity must have been ....

Writing skills

PART 2 A SHORT STORY

1 Read the question and one of the entries in the competition opposite and put the verbs in 1–12 into the correct past tense. Remember to use the past perfect for events which happened before others in the past.

2 Adverbs can make your writing more interesting. Underline the adverbs in the story.

3 Number events a–j in the order in which they take place in the story.

a The man began to stare in Mr Brown's direction.

b The train stopped.

c Mr Brown boarded the train.

d The man showed the attractive lady his police identification.

e The man arrested the dark-haired lady.

f Mr Brown read a headline in the newspaper.

g A famous painting was stolen.

h The attractive lady got up.

i The train left the station.

j The man asked if he could borrow the newspaper.

Interesting the reader

4 A successful short story holds the attention of the reader. Decide what the writer of the story opposite wants you to think, and say what is unexpected about the ending of the story.

The language of description

5 What are adjectives a–l used to describe in the story?

a black
b attractive
c suspicious
d old-fashioned
e grey
f large
g tall
h long
i happy
j uncomfortable
k thin
l dark-haired

You have decided to enter a short story competition in a local newspaper. The story must begin with these words:

The middle-aged man in the seat opposite Mr Brown looked suspicious.

The middle-aged man in the seat opposite Mr Brown looked suspicious. He was extremely tall and thin, and had a large, black moustache. He ¹ .... (wear) a long, grey raincoat and an old-fashioned hat. He ² .... (stare) in Mr Brown's direction ever since the train ³ .... (leave) the station. Mr Brown, who ⁴ .... (work) busily on his laptop computer, ⁵ .... (begin) to feel slightly uncomfortable.

The man suddenly ⁶ .... (lean) across and asked Mr Brown if he could borrow his newspaper. Mr Brown reluctantly ⁷ .... (give) it to him. He

6 The words in descriptions a–d are in the wrong order. Put them in the correct order.

a leather jacket a short brown

   ....

b a(n) ring diamond expensive-looking

   ....

c vase blue Indian a(n)

   ....

d beautiful with hair a long young woman

   ....

⁸.................. (not/finish) reading it himself. He
⁹.................. (see) only the headline about the theft of a famous painting before boarding the train.

The attractive, dark-haired lady sitting next to him with her large briefcase was a completely different matter. Mr Brown would have been happy to be stared at by her. The train ¹⁰.................. (stop) abruptly. The lady hurriedly ¹¹.................. (get) up but the man ¹².................. (stand up), blocking the doorway.
'Not so fast,' he said, showing her his police identification.
'I'm arresting you for the theft of a Picasso painting from the National Museum last night.'

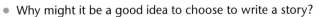
Paper 2 Part 2

Answer these questions.

- Why might it be a good idea to choose to write a story?
- What should you do before starting to write?
- What kind of sentences should you try to write?
- How can you highlight the most interesting part of the story?

The verb *look*

7 The man in the story *looked suspicious*. Match the examples of the verb *look* in a–h with meanings 1–8.

a The hotel *was not much to look at* but the staff were friendly.

b Since winning the talent competition, Susan has *never looked back*.

c You should *look after* yourself instead of thinking about other people.

d It's difficult for the company to *look ahead* at the moment.

e Don't *look round,* but I think that's someone famous over there.

f Don't you think John's beginning to *look his age*?

g I *don't like the look of* that cut. I think you should see a doctor.

h *Look out!* That car's going fast!

1 after one success become more successful
2 take care of
3 think about what might happen in the future
4 be worried by the appearance of something
5 seem as old as you really are
6 be careful
7 turn your head in order to see something
8 not attractive in appearance

8 Insert these adverbs in a suitable place in sentences a–h in 7. More than one answer may be possible.

> straightaway   immediately   much too
> always   incredibly   really   actually

Writing a story

9 You have decided to enter a short story competition in a magazine. The story must be 120–180 words and begin with these words:

> *The lady at the end of the ticket queue looked worried.*

Include some adverbs and adjectives. The Writing checklist will help you.

Writing checklist

Reader able to visualise the places and people	☐
Adjectives and adverbs included	☐
Story not too complicated	☐
The right length	☐
Legible handwriting	☐

Use of English skills

PART 5 WORD FORMATION

1 Read the main text quickly and decide whether the writer is being serious or amusing.

fashion in sport

My sister is working at the Commonwealth Games and has to wear chinos, a T-shirt and a bumbag – totally ⁰ _undesirable_ for a 21-year-old. But fashion has never been sport's priority – those who take part in ¹ .... want their bodies to be streamlined for the sake of aerodynamics. So most clothes worn at the games by staff and ² .... are awful. Athletes actually wear the only truly modern clothes – this is because of all the ³ .... advances in the manufacture of fabrics designed to improve sporting ⁴ .... Modern clothes have benefited enormously from the ⁵ .... of nylon and lycra, but most of the new man-made fabrics do not lend themselves to being turned into ⁶ .... fashions. Sportswear needs to find a way to make athletes look ⁷ .... , and aerodynamic, too. Not all the clothes modelled at the games were ⁸ .... , however. There were a few exceptions of good taste, as well as examples of a terrible lack of ⁹ .... by those wearing the clothes. But this is my advice to anyone who wants to look ¹⁰ .... : remember that it is not what you wear but the way you wear it that counts.

DESIRE

ATHLETE
COMPETE

TECHNOLOGY
PERFORM
INTRODUCE
STYLE
ATTRACT
DISASTER

JUDGE
FASHION

2 For questions 1–10 in 1, use the word given in capitals at the end of each line to form a word that fits in the space in the same line.

CHECK

Noun endings

3 Turn verbs a–h into nouns using the endings below. Some of the verbs are from the text. You may need to change or add letters. Which two verbs can be made into nouns describing a thing and a person?

Verb	Noun		Verb	Noun
a know	....		e realise	....
b mean	....		f perform	....
c remain	....		g compete	....
d attract	....		h win	....

-y   -er   -ing   -ity   -edge   -ion   -ment   -ance   -or

REPORTED SPEECH

Test your knowledge

Correct these sentences.

a My brother asked me I wanted to go to the cinema.
b Our neighbour suggested us to go to Italy on holiday.
c A lady asked me what time did the show end.
d Mark apologised me for being late.
e Dr Smedley asked me weather I exercised regularly.
f Kate asked me if I had saw the film already.

Reporting imperatives

4 Say which of sentences a and b is more polite and what you think the fashion designer actually said each time.

a The fashion designer told the models to walk slowly.
b The fashion designer asked the models to walk slowly.

5 Report sentences a–e beginning with the words in brackets and using either *asked* or *told*.

a 'Please don't forget to get your clothes ready for school.' (Ben's mother ...)
b 'Choose the pair of jeans you like best!' (The children's aunt ...)
c 'Come shopping with me.' (My friend ...)
d 'Never buy uncomfortable shoes!' (My sister ...)
e 'Could you use cubicle number six to try the dress on, madam?' (The sales assistant ...)

Reporting statements

6 When reporting what people say, you usually need to change the tense of the verb in the statement you are reporting. Turn a–e into reported statements, making the appropriate changes.

a 'The city's fashion week will finish tomorrow,' said an official.

....

b 'The designers have travelled here from all over the world,' said the reporter.

....

c 'The designs have been exciting up to now,' said a spectator.

....

d 'I won a fashion award yesterday,' said John.

....

e 'All the models are wearing the latest designs today,' said a reporter.

....

Exam know-how

Paper 3 Part 5
Complete the missing information.

● You should read the text .... after reading it first quickly for overall meaning.
● You might need to add .... to the word in capitals.
● The correct spelling is ....
● You should look at the context to see if the word you need is .... in meaning.

7 If what is reported is still true, and/or the speaker uses a reporting verb in the present, it is not usually necessary to change the tense of the verbs in the statements. Report quotes a–d from the text, making any necessary changes to pronouns and possessive adjectives, and begining with the words given.

a 'My sister is working at the Commonwealth Games and has to wear chinos.'
   The writer said ....

b 'Athletes actually wear the only truly modern clothes.'
   The writer says ....

c 'Ready-to-wear fashions have benefited enormously from the introduction of nylon and lycra.'
   The writer says ....

d 'There were a few exceptions of good taste.'
   The writer said ....

Reporting questions

8 When you report questions, you have to change the order of the words in the direct question. Complete the missing information in reported questions a–e. What word do you need to add in c and d?

a Where is the fashion show?
   Pat asked a passer-by where ....
b How long have you been working for this company?
   The reporter asked Claire how long ....
   ....
c Are you interested in sports fashion?
   The reporter asked me.. .
d Are you going to buy a new outfit for the party?
   Ian asked me ....
e What time does the show end?
   The woman asked the man next to her ....
   ....

Listening skills

PART 4 A CHOICE OF TWO OPTIONS
Different spellings, similar sounds

1 In English, the same sound can be spelt in different ways. Match 1–10 from the recording in 2 with words a–j which they rhyme with.

1	funny	a	flower
2	sort	b	trial
3	sleep	c	fork
4	night	d	heap
5	our	e	write
6	walk	f	stuff
7	while	g	taught
8	tough	h	cake
9	though	i	slow
10	break	j	money

2 🎧 You will hear Bob and Mary, a husband and wife comedy team, being interviewed on the radio. For questions 1–7, decide which views are expressed by any of the speakers and which are not. Write **YES** next to those views that are expressed and **NO** next to those which are not.

1 Bad jokes are often amusing. ....

2 You need a particular talent to be good at comedy. ....

3 Success in comedy is easier than in other kinds of acting. ....

4 Opportunities in life often come about unexpectedly. ....

5 Members of Parliament are boring to listen to. ....

6 Touring is one of the most exciting times in a actor's life. ....

7 Sometimes it's difficult to find the right kind of material for comedy. ....

What about you?

3 Answer these questions.

a What kind of comedy shows do you find funny? Why?

b What other kinds of TV programmes attract large audiences in your country?

Speaking skills

PARTS 3 AND 4 THE COLLABORATIVE TASK AND DISCUSSION (A GROUP OF 3)

1 Put inventions 1–6 in the order in which you think they were invented beginning with the oldest. If you were given these pictures in the exam, what do you think the examiner might ask you to talk about?

Exam know-how

Paper 5 Part 4
Answer these questions.
- Why are short answers not suitable for Part 4?
- Why is it important not to talk across your partner?
- When should you **not** answer a question?
- What should you be prepared to use when answering Part 4 questions?

2 Read the Part 3 task on page 116, then try to remember what you have to do. How long do the three of you have to do the task?

3 Do the task in 2 together in the time allowed, using the visuals in 1 and some of the phrases below.

CHECK

Inviting both partners to speak

What do you both think about … ?

Have either of you anything else to say about … ?

What about you two? What do you think?

Interrupting politely

Actually, I'd just like to say …

Sorry to interrupt but …

Could I just say that … ?

4 Answer these questions.
- a What other modern inventions have changed the way we live?
- b What new thing would you like to invent if you could?
- c Do you think in future people will do more, or less, travelling?
- d Many people now work from an office at home. Is this a good idea?
- e Do you think people are happier now than they were in the past?

Revise and extend

Phrasal verbs with *cut*

▶ Revision p95 Ex5

1 Match phrasal verbs a–d with meanings 1–4.

a cut off	1 interrupt
b cut out	2 omit/remove
c cut in	3 disconnect
d cut back on	4 reduce

▶ Extension p95 Ex5

2 Match the parts of the sentences, then match the verbs with *cut* with their meanings 1–4.

a We protested about the number of trees they ...

b This new organisation for helping children ...

c After the widespread floods, the villagers ...

d The cake will be easier to serve if we ...

... cut it up first.

... were going to cut down.

... were cut off.

... cuts across national differences.

1 is not restricted by

2 make fall by cutting

3 prevent from leaving or having contact

4 divide into pieces

3 Use the phrasal verbs from 2 to complete sentences a–d.

a This international sports organisation .... all differences in race or nationality.

b When he was working abroad he felt .... from his friends and family.

c Have you got a sharp knife to .... the pizza .... ?

d I think we should .... that old oak tree. It looks dangerous to me.

Words connected with feeling well or unwell

▶ Extension p94/5 Text

4 Say which of these words are normally used as a noun, as a verb, or both. Then match them with a–f.

> hurt   heal   harm   ache   pain   injury

a physical suffering (usually short and sharp)

b cause somebody or yourself physical pain

c physical suffering (usually long or continuous)

d become or make healthy again

e what can happen as the result of an accident

f cause damage

Words with *ache*

▶ Extension p94/95 Text

5 Use one of the words in 4 in its correct form to complete sentences a–f. More than one answer may be possible.

a I've got a terrible .... in my wrist.

b That cut will .... itself if you leave it alone!

c My legs are .... after all that running.

d Surely one little bar of chocolate can do no .... ?

e Only one of the passengers suffered minor .... in the train crash.

f If I press your arm here, does it .... ?

6 We use the noun *ache* with some parts of the body, e.g. *toothache*. Decide which of a–k can be used with *ache*.

a foot	g ear
b back	h neck
c chest	i head
d stomach	j heart
e arm	k heel
f knee	

Writing

▶ Extension p94/95

7 A TV programme is offering viewers the chance to do any job of their choice for a week. Write a paragraph explaining what job you would most like to do and why you should be one of the winners.

Reported speech

▶ Revision p99

8 Change sentences a–j into direct speech.

a Alex said he had just bought a smart navy suit.

b The manager told the sales assistant to try to be more helpful to customers.

c Anna said she had never won an award for fashion before.

d Peter asked if anyone had seen his sports bag.

e The reporter asked if anyone in the audience was prepared to take part in a fashion competition.

f The guests commented that all the models were looking very elegant.

g Journalists asked the award winners if they would pose for a group photo.

h The announcer said that the next show would take place in half an hour.

i The men complained that they couldn't see any designs they wanted to wear.

j The organisers asked the cameramen to stop making so much noise.

9 Decide which of 1–6 are followed by constructions a–d when used to report speech.

a the infinitive form, e.g. *to do*

b *whether*, *if* or a question word

c *that* + another sentence

d the *-ing* form of the verb

1 suggested   4 complained

2 threatened   5 offered

3 wondered   6 wanted to know

10 Use one of the verbs in 9 followed by the correct construction to report sentences a–f. The words in brackets will help you.

a 'Can anyone afford to buy these designer clothes?' (a fashion photographer)

b 'I can't see anything from where I'm sitting'. (one reporter)

c 'I'll get you a programme'. (the woman sitting next to me)

d 'I'm going home if the models don't appear in something more interesting!' (one fashion writer)

e 'Let's all sit nearer the front.' (one of the guests)

f 'How many people do you think there are in the hall?' (a friend)

Key word transformations

▶ Revision p99

11 For questions a–f, complete the second sentence so that it has a similar meaning to the first sentence, using the word given. Do not change the word given. You must use between two and five words, including the word given.

a 'Please don't make a noise in the library,' said the librarian to Jim.
   asked
   The librarian .... a noise in the library.

b 'Dinner will be served at 7 o'clock,' the hotel manager said to us.
   informed
   The hotel manager .... be served at 7 o'clock.

c 'Are you interested in the theatre?' my aunt said to me.
   if
   My aunt asked .... interested in the theatre.

d 'How does Jane feel about the decision we made yesterday?' Sally asked.
   know
   Sally wanted .... about the decision made the day before.

e 'What about going for a picnic?' my mother said to us.
   suggested
   My mother .... go for a picnic.

f 'You have passed the exam,' said the teacher to me.
   told
   The teacher .... passed the exam.

Grammar reference

MODULE 1a

Negative prefixes (page 4)

We can use prefixes like *un, im, in, dis*, to make the meaning of words negative. We use:

im before the letters *b, m* and *p*, e.g. *imbalance, immature, impossible.*

il before the letter *l*, e.g. *illegal.*

ir before the letter *r*, e.g. *irresponsible.*

un is a very common negative prefix, e.g. *unnecessary, unhappy.*

Can you tell me ... (page 7)

The word order in questions of this type is reversed to subject + verb (not verb + subject).

'Are you coming by train?'
Could you let me know if you are coming by train?

'Where is the station?'
Could you tell me where the stadium is?

Modals (page 8)

1 can/could are used:

a to say that someone knows how to do something.
  Sam could speak two languages when he was only six.
b to make a polite request.
  Could/Can you help me with this suitcase?
c to make a suggestion.
  We could/can meet for a coffee tomorrow if you like.
d to ask for permission informally.
  Could/Can I use your phone?
e to talk about a possibility.
  What Teresa said could be true.
f to talk about ability.
  Can you meet me at the station?

2 be able to is used:

a to say that someone knows how to do something.
  Tina is able to fly an aeroplane.
b to talk about ability.
  Are you able to come to the party tomorrow night?

3 may/might (not) are used:

a to talk about a possibility.
  It may/might be a fine day tomorrow.
b to ask for permission formally.
  May/Might I ask a question?
  You may leave the room for a few minutes.
c *may* can be used to give permission formally.
  You may leave the room for a few minutes.

4 must be/have been, can't be/have been are used:

a to say you are certain that something is true.
  Simon must be tired after running in the marathon.
  Edward must have been exhausted after all that hard work.
b to say that you are certain that something is not true.
  Claudia can't be Tim's new girlfriend. She's going out with me!
  Celia can't have been at home last night. No-one answered when I phoned.

5 should/ought to do (have done) are used:

a to say that it is right or wrong to do something.
  You should/ought to let your parents know where you are.
  We shouldn't/ought not to have spent so much money.
b to say that something will almost certainly happen/has almost certainly happened.
  We should/ought to arrive home about 10 o'clock if the traffic isn't too heavy.
  The plane should/ought to have taken off by now.

6 must/mustn't are used:

a to say that it is important (not) to do something.
  I must remember to post that letter!
b to say it is wrong to do something, or something is forbidden.
  You mustn't tell lies.
  Students mustn't smoke in the classrooms.

7 (not) have/had to are used:

a to talk about an obligation.
  Robert has to be at work early tomorrow morning.
  We had to write two compositions in class last week.
b to talk about a lack of obligation.
  We don't have to go to school tomorrow. It's Sunday.
  I didn't have to hand in any homework yesterday. The teacher didn't give us any.

8 didn't need to (do)/needn't have (done) are used:

a use *didn't need to* to talk about what it was not necessary to do, and *which* you may or may not have done.
  We didn't need to get up early so we stayed in bed until 11 o'clock.
b to talk about something that it was not necessary to do, but which you did.
  We needn't have arrived at the airport so early because the plane was delayed.

MODULE 1b

The future (page 19)

1 *Going (to do)* is used:

a to talk about an intention.
  I'm going to stay in tonight.

b to talk about a probability based on evidence now.
  It's going to be a nice day tomorrow.

2 The present continuous is used:

  to talk about a definite future arrangement.
  I'm having a job interview on Thursday.

3 *Will* **is used:**

a to express a willingness or offer to do something.
  I'll help you with your homework.

b to make a request.
  Will you help me with the washing up?

c to make an immediate decision.
  I'll phone for a taxi!

d to make a promise.
  I won't let you down!

e to express determination.
  I will pass my driving test!

f to make a prediction.
  It will be spring soon.

g to express an inability or refusal to do something.
  This key won't turn in the lock.
  I won't forgive you for what you said!

4 *shall* **is used:**

a to make a suggestion.
  Shall we go for a pizza?

b to make an offer.
  Shall I post those letters for you?

5 The simple present is used:

  to talk about a future event, e.g. on a timetable.
  The summer holidays begin on Friday.

6 The future continuous is used:

  To talk about an action which will be taking place at a certain time in the future.
  This time next week, we'll be travelling to Switzerland.

7 The future perfect is used:

  To talk about an action which will be finished before a certain time in the future.
  I'll have finished this homework by 6 o'clock.

Other ways of talking about the future

be about to, be on the point of (*be ready to*) and *be due to* (*be expected to*) can also be used to talk about the future.

I was about to give Dave a call, when the phone rang.
We were on the point of leaving when some unexpected guests arrived.
The plane is due to take off in ten minutes' time.

Adjectives + prepositions/Verbs + the *–ing* form of the verb (page 21)

The *–ing* form of the verb is used:

a after an adjective followed by a preposition.
  I'm not very fond of reading.
  I get fed up with listening to the radio.

b as the object of a verb.
  I like swimming.
  I can't stand playing football.

MODULE 2a

despite/in spite/although (page 27)

The meaning of these words is similar but they are used differently.

a We use *despite/in spite of* + a noun or the *–ing* form of the verb.
  Despite/In spite of the heat, we went for a walk.
  Despite/In spite of having no money, we had an enjoyable weekend.

b We use *although* + part of a sentence.
  Although it was late, we decided to go out for a meal.
  We went climbing although I didn't really want to go.

Using adverbs (page 28)

1 Adverbs are used:

  to describe most verbs and are also used to describe adjectives, participles and other adverbs.

adverb + verb	*Tania sings well.*
adverb + adjective	*The park is relatively big.*
adverb + participle	*These boats are very well made.*
adverb + adverb	*We found our way fairly easily.*

2 Adverbs can be placed:

a between the auxiliary verb and the main verb.
  I have always liked pizza.

b between the subject of a sentence and a regular verb.
  I never go to the theatre.

c after a verb like *to be*, or a modal.
  I am always late for school.
  You must never tell lies.

3 Adverbs of time (*sometimes, occasionally, generally,* etc.) can be used:

at the beginning of a sentence for emphasis.
Sometimes, I enjoy sports.

Using present tenses (page 28)

1 The present simple is used:

a to talk about things which happen regularly or are always true.
The sun sets in the west.

b with adverbs of time.
always, generally, usually, sometimes, hardly ever, never

c to talk about an event on a timetable.
The school term starts on the 8th January

2 The present continuous is used:

a to talk about things that are happening at the moment.
The children are playing in the garden.

b to talk about things that are happening over a longer period of time.
Interest rates are slowly falling.

c with *always* to talk about something that happens on a regular basis and can be annoying.
My brother is always borrowing my trainers.

3 Verbs rarely used in the present continuous

Verbs which refer to states or conditions, not actions, are rarely used in the continuous form. Here are some examples.

Verbs of feeling
like, dislike, love, hate, need, want, prefer

Verbs of appearance
appear, seem

Verbs of possession
own, belong to, have

Verbs of physical perception
hear, smell, see, taste

Verbs of thinking
know, realize, suppose, understand, believe

The passive (page 29)

The passive is used:

a when we are more interested in the subject of the sentence than in who did the action.
The ship was built in Norway.

b when we do not know who did the action.
My car was stolen last week.

c when the action and the person who did the action are important.
An announcement was made by the ship's captain.

d in newspaper reports.
Two passengers were injured in a coach accident last night.

e to describe scientific experiments or processes.
The mixture was heated slowly.

f to describe what people think generally.
It is known that physical exercise is good for the health.

g it is obvious or unimportant who does the action.
Our instructors are given the best training possible.

had better (page 32)

had better (do) means 'it would be better if (you) did'.
We had better order a taxi.
You'd better ring for an ambulance.

bound and *likely* (to) (page 32)

a Bound to means 'certain to happen'
It's bound to rain tomorrow.
We're bound to miss the plane if we don't hurry.

b Likely to means 'there is a good chance of this happening'
It's likely to be a difficult journey.

❶ *Likely* can be used as an adjective with the same meaning as *likely to* but *bound to* cannot be used in this way.

They say it's going to be a hot summer but I don't think that's very likely, do you?

Infinitive forms
The infinitive can be used in different forms.

to teach

to be taught (passive)

to be teaching (continuous)

MODULE2b

Talking about past experiences (page 38)

1 The simple past is used:

a to talk about completed actions in the past.
I spent several months in Italy in 2002.

b with expressions that refer to points of time.
yesterday morning, last month, at midnight, on Sunday, in June, two weeks ago, the day before yesterday, when I was a teenager

c to describe a number of actions happening one after the other.
I got up early, had breakfast and caught the train.

2 The past continuous is used:

a to talk about things that were happening when another action took place.
I was driving to work when I heard the news.

b to set the scene in a story.
We were canoeing down the river and the sun was shining.

3 *used to* (+ infinitive) is used:

a to describe past habits.
I used to go to the cinema twice a week.

b to talk about an action which didn't happen in the past but does now.
I didn't use to like going to the theatre.

c to describe past states or conditions.
The days used to seem longer when I was a child.

❶ *would* can also be used instead of *used to* but it cannot be used to describe a state or condition, only an action.

My aunt would/used to feed the chickens every morning.
She used to be a quiet sort of person.

4 *To be used to* (+ *-ing*) is used:

to talk about an action which you were accustomed to doing.

The children were used to travelling long distances by car.

5 *To get used to* (+ *-ing*) is used:

to talk about an action which you became accustomed to doing.

It was hard work but we soon got used to canoeing through the waves.

Comparing adjectives and adverbs (page 41)

a Most single-syllable adjectives and adverbs are compared using *-er* and *-est*.
old, older, the oldest
hard, harder, the hardest

b Two syllable adjectives ending in *-y*, e.g. *friendly, wealthy, easy* and some others, e.g. *clever, quiet, narrow* also follow this pattern.
Last week's test was much easier.
My brother is cleverer than I am.

c Most other adjectives and adverbs with two or more syllables are compared with *more, the most*.
Tigers are dangerous animals.
Lions are more dangerous than tigers.
Hungry lions are the most dangerous animals of all.

d We can also make negative comparisons with adjectives and adverbs using *not as ... as*.
I do not speak English as fluently as my sister.

e Irregular comparatives and superlatives. The most common of these are:
good/better/best (adjective)
well/better/best (adverb)
bad/worse/the worst (adjective)
badly/worse/the worst (adverb)

f The present perfect is often used with superlatives.
She is the nicest person I have ever met.

MODULE3a

Making suggestions and recommendations

The verbs *suggest* and *recommend* are used:

a with *that*.
I suggest/recommend that you go to university.
They suggested/recommended that I went to university.

b with the *-ing* form of the verb.
I suggest painting the room blue.
I recommend painting the room blue.

❶ When *suggest* is followed by the *-ing* form of the verb, the speaker is including him/herself in the suggested activity.

Paul suggested going to the cinema.

Present perfect tense (page 48)

1 The present perfect simple is used:

a to talk about a non-specific time in the past, i.e. when no time is mentioned.
I've bought a new bicycle.

b to talk about a present situation which is the result of a previous action.
You've torn your jacket.

c with adverbs of time, e.g. *just* (recently), *already* (before now), *still*, *yet*:

already/just
Have you (already) seen this film (already)?
Yes, we've just finished watching it.

still (to talk about an ongoing situation)
The programme still hasn't finished.
Has the programme still not finished?

yet (this hasn't happened, but is expected to)
Has the film finished yet?
I haven't done my homework yet.

ever (at any time up to the present)
Have you ever been to Spain?

never (at no time in the past) – to talk about personal experience
I've never been to a disco.

d with prepositions or prepositional phrases, e.g. *this morning/week, so far, up to now*, to talk about actions which are still going on or which have just finished.
We've studied two different books this term.
I've worked hard over the last two days.

e with *been* and *gone* to convey a different meaning.
Ben has been to Madrid. (He is not there now.)
Ben has gone to Madrid. (He is there now).

f with *for* and *since* to talk about how long something has lasted and when it began.
Ben has worked here for two months.
Ben has been here since the end of last month.

g with *the first/second*, or a superlative.
This is the third time I've been to this night club.
Ben is the best DJ I have ever seen.

2 The present perfect continuous

The present perfect continuous is used:

a to emphasise the length of an action, which may still be going on.
Ben has been rehearsing for hours!
Ben has been rehearsing since 8.30 this morning.

b to express anger or irritation at the length of time an action has taken
I've been trying to phone you all morning!

MODULE 3b

Emphasising a point (page 56)

What can be used to mean the thing(s) that to emphasise a point at the beginning of the sentence or after a verb as the object of a sentence.

What annoyed me was the way he spoke to the teacher.
I don't understand what you are talking about.

Relative clauses and pronouns (page 58)

1 Defining relative clauses

Defining relative clauses make it clear which person or thing we are talking about.

a We use relative pronouns such as *who, which, where* or *that* to refer to people or things.
The director who/that made this film is very well known.
This is the place where Shakespeare was born.

b The relative pronoun can be left out if it is the object of a verb.
This is the book (–) I was talking about yesterday.

c The relative pronoun *whose* refers to possession.
I met an artist whose work is famous.

d *Whom* can be used as an object pronoun referring to a person, but *who* or *that* are also acceptable.
The man who(m)/that I talked to was very interesting.

e If the relative pronoun comes after a preposition such as *to, from, with,* etc. *whom* must be used.
The student who I was talking to was very intelligent.
The student to whom I was talking was very intelligent.

2 Non-defining relative clauses

Non-defining relative clauses contain additional information about a person or thing already mentioned.

a Commas are always used around the non-defining relative clause.

b The pronoun cannot be left out and it is not possible to use *that*.

c You can use *which* to refer to things, *when* to refer to time, *where* to refer to place.
My notebook, which was here a minute ago, seems to have disappeared.
The winter, when the weather is severe, is not a good time to visit Alaska.
Every summer I go to the beach, where my parents have a caravan.

MODULE 4a

Using adverbs (page 65)

Formation

a Most adverbs are formed by adding *-ly* to the adjective.
free, freely

b Some adverbs have the same form as the adjective.
hard, fast, early, late, far

c Some adverbs are very different from the adjectival form.
good – well

d Some adjectives ending in *-ly* do not have a corresponding adverb.
friendly, lonely, silly, elderly

If we want to use them as adverbs, we have to rephrase the sentence.

She smiled at me in a friendly way.

Gerunds and prepositions (page 66)

If we want to use a verb form after a preposition, we use the gerund.

I am not keen on listening to the radio.

Past perfect tense (page 69)

1 The past perfect simple is used:

a in a sentence usually containing another verb in the past simple, for an action which happened before another in the past.
The miners had been underground for almost two days when they were rescued.

b to report a verb in the present perfect or simple past in indirect speech.
'I've never been on a cruise before,' said my aunt.
My aunt said that she had never been on a cruise before.

'I visited a friend in hospital once,' said my aunt.
My aunt said she had visited a friend in hospital once.

2 The past perfect continuous is used:

a in a sentence usually containing another verb in the past simple, for an action which had been happening before another in the past.

One miner, who had been working near the surface of the mine, managed to escape.

The rescue team had been working for several hours when they heard the sound of voices.

b to report a verb in the present perfect continuous or past continuous in indirect speech.

'I've been looking after the injured miners,' said my uncle.

My uncle said that he had been looking after the injured miners.

'I was watching TV when I heard the news,' said my uncle.

My uncle said he had been watching TV when he heard the news.

MODULE4b

Conditionals (page 79)

a The zero conditional: *if* + present tense, + present tense. This is used when *if* means 'whenever' or 'every time'.

If people drink too quickly, they often get hiccups.

b The first conditional: *if* + present simple or continuous, or present perfect tense, *will* or a modal, e.g. *may, can, must,* + infinitive.

This is used to talk about things which might happen in the future.

If you go out in this rain, you'll get soaked.

If you're not doing anything, would you help me with the vegetables?

If you've finished doing your homework, we can go to the cinema.

c The second conditional: *if* + past simple or continuous, *would* or a modal, e.g. *might/could,* + infinitive. This is used to talk about imaginary or unlikely situations, and to give advice.

If I were a film star, I would be famous.

If I were you, I'd take a break from studying.

d The third conditional: *if* + past perfect simple or continuous, *would have* or a modal, e.g. *might, could,* + the past participle of the verb. This is used to speculate about what happened in the past.

If I had been at home, I would have answered your call.

If we hadn't won the lottery, we couldn't have gone on holiday.

If I hadn't been working on the computer, I might have heard the doorbell ring.

unless and in case

a *Unless* means 'if not'.

He would not ring at this time of night unless it was important.

b *In case* is quite different from *if*. *If* is used to explain that you do one thing if another happens.

If I have time, I'll go to the library.

In case is used to explain that you do something because you think something particular may happen.

I'll take my mobile phone, in case I need to contact you urgently.

Adjectives ending in -ed and -ing (page 82)

Adjectives ending in -ed are used:

to describe feelings.

I was bored by the film.

We weren't interested in listening to his excuses for being late.

Adjectives ending in -ing are used:

to describe the quality of something or somebody.

The story was interesting.

He was a very interesting man.

MODULE5a

before, after, when, while + -ing (page 87)

Instead of using a subordinate clause, e.g. *Before I finished, While I was studying,* we can use *before, after, when, while* + -*ing*.

While spending a holiday in the Mediterranean, we met an old friend.

The subject of the other part of the sentence must be the same as the unmentioned subject of the -*ing* form of the verb.

While cycling home, Bob got a flat tyre.

regret (doing)/regret (to do) (page 89)

Some verbs change their meaning depending whether they are followed by the gerund or the infinitive.

a We use the -*ing* form after some verbs, e.g. *regret doing/remember doing,* when we are sorry about, or haven't forgotten what we did.

I regret telling Angela about the party.

I remember visiting this place when I was a child.

b We use the infinitive with *to* after some verbs, e.g. *regret to tell/remember to tell,* when we are sorry about or remember what we are about to do.

I regret to say that I did not find what you said amusing.

Please remember to post my letter.

Verbs followed by *-ing* or the infinitive

1 Verbs + *-ing* form

a A number of common verbs and expressions are usually followed by the *-ing* form rather than the infinitive.
I enjoy travelling.

Other common verbs that follow this pattern are:
appreciate, avoid, can't help, can't stand, consider, deny, dislike, enjoy, feel like, finish, give up, it's not worth , it's no use, keep on, look forward to, mention, mind, miss, object to, practise, put off, risk, suggest, there's no point
(Remember that all verbs usually take the *-ing* form after a preposition.)

b Some verbs are followed by an object + preposition + *-ing* form.
May I congratulate you on winning this award.

Other common verbs that follow this pattern are:
apologise to somebody for, accuse somebody of, blame somebody for, prevent somebody from, protect somebody from, thank somebody for.

2 Verbs + infinitive

a Some verbs are followed by the infinitive rather than the *-ing* form.
I want to stay in and watch a film on TV tonight.

Other common verbs that follow this pattern are:

afford, appear, arrange, decide, expect, fail, happen, hope, intend, learn, manage, offer, plan, prepare, pretend, promise, refuse, seem, threaten, want

b *Make* and *let* are followed by an infinitive without *to*.
They made me play games every afternoon.

c Some verbs are followed by an object + infinitive.
Ted has asked me to go to the cinema on Saturday night.

Other common verbs that follow this pattern are:

advise, allow, enable, encourage, force, invite, order, persuade, remind, teach, tell

3 Verbs + *-ing* or + infinitive

a Some verbs can be followed by either the *-ing* form or infinitive, and there is no difference in meaning.
We started to revise/revising for our exams last month.

Other verbs like this are:
begin, intend, continue

b Verbs of perception (*see, hear, watch*, etc.) are usually followed by the *-ing* form if we see part of the action, and by the infinitive if we see all of the action.
I saw the horses running across the field.
(I noticed that they were there.)

I saw Tim Henman play against a tough opponent yesterday.
(I saw the whole tennis match.)

c Some verbs change in meaning when followed by the *-ing* form or infinitive.
I like going for a swim. (I enjoy doing it.)
I like to go for a swim once a week. (I choose to do it.)

Wishes and regrets (page 89)

I wish/If only are used:

a to express regret about a present situation. We use *I wish/If only* + the past form of the verb.
I wish I could come with you on holiday.
If only I was/were better at languages.

b to express regret about a past action. We use *I wish/If only* + the past perfect.
I wish I hadn't bought those shoes.
If only I had listened to my mother.

c to complain about someone's behaviour. We use *I wish/If only* + *would* (*not*) + infinitive.
I wish Michael wouldn't leave his dirty clothes on the floor.
I wish you wouldn't make that noise.

❶ We never say 'I wish I would', we say 'I wish I could'.

Reflexive and emphasising pronouns (page 92)

1 Reflexive pronouns

These pronouns, *myself, yourself, him/herself, ourselves, yourselves, themselves,* are used when the object of the verb refers back to the subject, e.g. *serve yourself, help ourselves.* They cannot be separated from the verb they belong to.

2 Emphasising pronouns

These are the same as reflexive pronouns but they are used to stress that someone did something on their own, without help. They follow the object of the verb:

I wrote this essay myself.

They are often used with *by*:

Sam decorated this room all by himself.

MODULE 5b

The order of adjectives (page 96)

When two or more adjectives appear before a noun, we put them in this order:

Your opinion	Lovely
size/weight	long
age	old
shape	square
colour	red
country of origin	Chinese
material	silk
noun	scarf

❶ Do not try to use too many adjectives before a noun. Two or three are usually enough.

Reporting questions (page 99)

a The tense changes in reported questions are exactly the same as in reported speech.

b When reporting direct questions, we use the word *if* or *whether* before the question.
Did you arrive late?
She asked me if I had arrived late.

c When reporting a question which begins with a question word, e.g. *who, which, where, why, when, how,* we repeat the question word.
Where did you buy the tracksuit?
He asked me where I had bought the tracksuit.

d The word order in reported questions is reversed to subject + verb (not verb + subject).
'Are you hungry?' (Robin)
Robin wondered if we were hungry.

❶ Question marks are not used in reported questions.

e Double questions also reverse order in this way.
Could you tell me where the stadium is?

Reported speech (page 99)

1 Leaving the tense unchanged

There is no need to make any tense changes if the reporting verb is in the present tense and the statement is still true.

'I love sports clothes.' (my sister)
My sister says she loves sports clothes.

2 Making tense changes

If the reporting verb is in the past tense, we usually have to change the tenses.

Actual words	Reported speech
Imperative *'Don't forget!'*	Infinitive *She told him not to forget.*
Simple present *'I am late.'*	Simple past *He said he was late.*
Present continuous *'She's wearing jeans.'*	Past continuous *They said she was wearing jeans.*
Simple past *'The manager phoned.'*	Past perfect *He said that the manager had phoned.*
Past continuous *'We were shopping for shoes.'*	Past perfect continuous *They said that they had been shopping for shoes.*
Present perfect simple *'No one has phoned.'*	Past perfect simple *She said that no one had phoned.*
Present perfect continuous *'Tim's been working too hard.'*	Past perfect continuous *She said Tim had been working too hard.*
Past perfect *'I had never been there before.'*	Past perfect (no change) *He said that he had never been there before.*

3 Other changes to make

If dates and times and places have been mentioned, make the following changes.

today	– that day
yesterday	– the day before/the previous day
tomorrow	– the next day/the following day/theday after
here	– there
this restaurant	– that restaurant

Phrasal verb alphabetical index

Separable phrasal verbs

NB When the object is a pronoun, it comes before the particle, or second part of the phrasal verb.

Non-separable phrasal verbs

Phrasal verbs with no object

Speaking skills appendix

MODULE2b page 41 2

I'd like you to compare and contrast these photographs and say why you think the people are in a hurry.

MODULE2b page 41 3

🎧 *First candidate:*

In this picture I can see a man who run for a train and he is in a hurry – yes ... . In the other picture I see a man ... er ... he eat breakfast in a hurry. Yes. He is hurry, too. I think they are hurry because they are late. Yes ... they are really late for something. They are late for work maybe. That's all!

Second candidate:

Well, both these pictures show people in a hurry. I think these people are rushing because ... er, well, they ... because they are late for something. In the first picture, the man is in a rush – in a hurry. He is eating his breakfast very quickly. It's not a good idea to eat breakfast quickly. But maybe he got up late because his alarm clock didn't go off – or he forgot to put the alarm on, or something like that. Maybe he went to bed late because he was – er watching television. In the second picture, I think the man is running for the train because he might be late for work, or he might have an important appointment – and it's important that he gets to the appointment in time. Maybe it's with his boss, so it's more important for him than it is for the man in this picture to be on time. Or maybe he needs the exercise.

MODULE3b page 61 2 3
Task 3

MODULE4a page 71 4

🎧 Examiner: What other kinds of things can make people happy?

Candidate 1:
Er ... . I don't know.

Candidate 2:
... other kinds of things? Well ... I think ... er ... maybe being famous! ... and success, too. That can make people happy. Perhaps passing an exam ... or getting good marks at school. I know that I feel happy when I do well at school.

Task 2

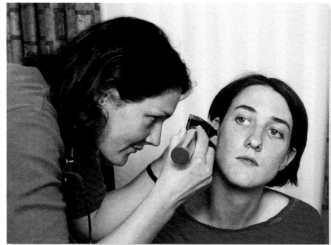

MODULE3a page 51 **4** **5**

Which job do you think looks more interesting?

MODULE5a page 91 **3** **4**

I'd like you to imagine that you are both going to work during your summer holidays to get some work experience. Here are some different places you can choose from. First, talk to each other about what qualities you would need to do the different jobs in these places. Then decide which place would be the most interesting to work in.

MODULE5b page 101 **2** **3**

Here are some pictures of important inventions. First, talk to each other about how these inventions have changed our lives. Then decide which three inventions have been the most important. You have only about four minutes for this.

MODULE4b page 81 5

1 What can we do to prevent certain kinds of animals dying out?

2 Where do you think airports should be built?

3 Some people say we should stop traffic from driving into city centres. Do you agree?

4 Instead of throwing things away, what could we do with them instead?

5 How can the different countries of the world help each other?

6 Do you think one day we might go and live on another planet? Why?

MODULE2b page 41 5

Task 1

These photographs show people taking exercise. I'd like you to compare and contrast these photographs, and say how you think the people are feeling.

MODULE3a page 51 4 5

Which job would you prefer to do?

Task 2

MODULE 2b page 41 **5**

Task 2

These photographs show people taking care of others. I'd like you to compare and contrast these photographs, and say why you think people choose to do jobs like these.

MODULE 4a page 71 **2** **3**

Now, I'd like you to talk together for about three minutes. I'm just going to listen. These pictures show things that can make people happy. First, talk to each other about how these things can make people happy. Then decide which two bring the most happiness.

MODULE 4b page 81 **2**

🎧 Now, I'd like you to talk together for about three minutes. I'm just going to listen. I'd like you to imagine that you are choosing two photographs to go on the cover of a book called *The World in Danger*. Here are some photographs to choose from. First, talk to each other about why the situations in these photographs are dangerous for the world. Then decide which two photographs should go on the cover of the book.

OXFORD
UNIVERSITY PRESS

Great Clarendon Street, Oxford OX2 6DP

Oxford University Press is a department of the University of Oxford. It furthers the University's objective of excellence in research, scholarship, and education by publishing worldwide in

Oxford New York

Auckland Bangkok Buenos Aires Cape Town Chennai
Dar es Salaam Delhi Hong Kong Istanbul Karachi Kolkata
Kuala Lumpur Madrid Melbourne Mexico City Mumbai
Nairobi São Paulo Shanghai Taipei Tokyo Toronto

Oxford and Oxford English are registered trade marks of Oxford University Press in the UK and in certain other countries

© Oxford University Press 2004

The moral rights of the author have been asserted

Database right Oxford University Press (maker)

First published 2004

ISBN 0 19 4386570

Printed in Hong Kong

Acknowledgements

p4 'If you go down to the woods ...' by Nigel Slater, *Observer Food Monthly*, June 2002 © Nigel Slater. Reproduced by permission.
p8 'X marks the empty spot in the BBC' by Martin Kelner, *The Guardian* 2 September 2002 © Guardian. Reproduced by permission.
p18 'Silent Spring' by Nicci Gerrard, *Observer* 21 March 1999 © Nicci Gerrard. Reproduced by permission
p24 *The Means of Escape* by Penelope Fitzgerald. Reprinted by permission of HarperCollins Publishers Ltd. © Penelope Fitzgerald.
p29 'Language cull could leave people speechless' by David Ward, *The Guardian* 25 May 2002 © Guardian. Reproduced by permission.
p34 *Rambling on the Road to Rome* by Peter Francis Browne. Reproduced by permission of Summersdale Publishers Ltd.
p36 Extract from 'The Stranger in the Mist' by A. N. L. Munby from *Oxford Bookworms 5: Ghost Stories retold by Rosemary Border*. Reproduced by permission of Sheila Munby,
p39 'Lapp it Up' by Sally Ramsden, *Livewire*, October/November 2000. Reproduced by permission of The Illustrated London News Picture Library.
p44 'The beats go on ...' by Alix Sharkey, *Observer Magazine*, 3 March 2002 © Alix Sharkey. Reproduced by permission.
p48 'New kid on the decks' by Giles Tremlett, *The Guardian* 26, March 2003 © Giles Tremlett. Reproduced by permission
p54 'I'm Britney, buy me' by Matthew Lynn, *British Airways Business Life*, April 2002 © Matthew Lynn. Reproduced by permission.
p58 'The History of the Iditarod' *CNN Traveller*, winter/spring 2001. Reproduced by permission.

p64 'One hell of a paradise' by Philip Moore, *British Airways High Life*, May 2002 © Philip Moore. Reproduced by permission.
p68 'Words that ended miners' three day ordeal ... what took you guys so long?' by Oliver Burkeman, *The Guardian*, 29 July 2002 © Guardian. Reproduced by permission.
p78 Adapted with permission from Children's Britannica, vol. 19 © 1997 by Encyclopædia Britannica, Inc.
p84 'Cheapness and Beauty' by Simon Calder, *British Airways High Life*, May 2002 © Simon Calder. Reproduced by permission.
p88 'There ain't no cure for the summertime blues' by Matt Robson-Scott, *The Guardian*, 24 July 2002 © Matt Robson-Scott. Reproduced by permission.
p94 'Accountant, heal thyself' by Frances Ive, *The Guardian*, 21 March 2002 © Frances Ive. Reproduced by permission.
p98 'And the fashion winners are ...' by Charlie Porter, *The Guardian*, 2 August 2002 © Guardian. Reproduced by permission.

Although every effort has been made to trace and contact copyright holders before publication, this has not been possible in some cases. We apologize for any apparent infringement of copyright and if notified, the publisher will be pleased to rectify any errors or omissions at the earliest opportunity.

The publishers and author would like to thank the following for their kind permission to reproduce photographs:

Alamy pp 84–5 (Eurostyle Graphics), 81 (Bryan & Cherry Alexander Photography/icebergh); Associated Press pp 40 (Jacques Brinon), 58 (Al Grillo), 68 (Guy Wathen), 98 (Richard Lewis/Beckham); BBC Photo Library pp 100, 116 (Parkinson), 117 (weather girl); Bryan and Cherry Alexander Photography p 29; Camera Press p 51 (Tina Paul/interviewing Ryan O'Neal), 117 (TSPL/Christopher Furlongsports commentator); John Cleare pp 34–35, 88; Corbis pp 5 (Georgia Lowell), 54–55 (Chuck Savage), 64 (Stephen Frink/turtle) 65 (Eye Ubiquitous/Bruce Adams/examining turtle/), 76–77 (Sygma/Flavio Pagini/country, Paul Almasy/city), 91 (Adam Woolfitt/cheese shop, Benjamin Rondel/collecting trolleys, Jose Luis Pelaez/filing, 118 (Ariel Skelley/orchestra, Robert Holmes/ski); Dance Picture Library/Linda Rich p 50, Getty Images pp 8 (Brett Froomer), 14 (Zane Williams), 18 (Geil), 30 (Daniel J. Cox), 31 (Martin Barraud/playing cards), 39 (Chad Ehlers), 41 Ghislain & Marie David de Lossy/breakfast and running, Loris Adamskie Peek/gym, Frank Herholdt/cyclists), 44–45 (Stephen Studd/river), 60 Walter Bibikow/landscape), 81 David Woodfall /landfill, R.G.K. Photography/forest, Ben Osbourne/bird, Chad Slattery /airport, Nello Giambi/car exhaust, 91 (Bluestone Productions/reception, Colin Hawkins/computer, Kyoko Hamada/photocopier); Peter Grant pp38–39; Katz Pictures pp91 (stacking shelves), 116 (printing room); Network Photographers pp 4 (Mike Goldwater), 51 (Roger Hutchings/Radio 4 studio), 61 (Martin Meyer/beach), 115 (Martin Meyer/bus queue), 116 (Martin Meyer/teacher); Photofusion pp 31 (Jacky Chapman/baby, Ulrike Preuss/blind man), 46 (David Tothill), 80 Crispin Hughes/doctors, D Christelis/teenage boys, Ulrike Preusse/bride), 91 Paul Doyle/checkout; Press Association pp 61 (Ben Curtis/Glastonbury), 81 (Peter Jordan/tigers), 98 (Jonathan Edwards); Rex Features pp 26 (Rex/New Line/Everett), 27 (Rex/Columbia/Everett), 31 (Stockbyte/disco), pp74–75 (Rex/Everett), 115 (EPA/airport queue); Science Photo Library pp70 (Martin Bond), 116 (Mark Thomas/doctor); Ski Shoot pp 91 (outside bar); Jens Stuart p 45 (Shakespeare & Co); Rod Westward p 49

Illustrations by:

Adrian Barclay pp 20, 21, 71
Paul Daviz pp 11, 90
Mark Duffin pp 24, 34, 46, 57, 67, 73, 78, 94, 101
John Haslam pp 5, 15
John Holder p 96–97
Alan Marks p 36–37
Patrick Morgan pp 16–17
John O'Leary pp 13, 23, 33, 43, 53, 63, 72, 83, 93, 102–103
Ian West pp 10, 86–87